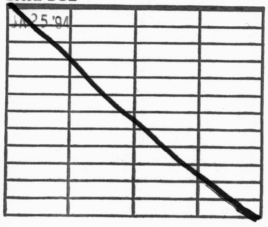

THE DOCTRINE OF JUDICIAL REVIEW

ITS LEGAL AND HISTORICAL BASIS AND OTHER ESSAYS

BY

EDWARD S. CORWIN

Of the Department of History and Politics, Princeton University

"The history of law must be a history of Ideas."—MAITLAND

GLOUCESTER, MASS.
PETER SMITH
1963

TO MY WIFE

PREFACE

In the preparation of another volume, not yet published, I have encountered a number of questions
involving controversies important to the student of
American Constitutional History, an extended consideration of which however in those pages I felt
to be out place. The following studies present my
conclusions with regard to these questions, and the
grounds of them. In the principal essay, I have endeavored to present judicial review as the outcome of a
view of *legislative* power which arose in consequence
of the astonishing abuse of their powers by the early
State legislatures but which was first appreciated for
its full worth by the Convention that framed the Constitution of the United States. Incidentally I have,
I trust, laid to rest that most inconclusive "explanation" of judicial review which dwells on the idea that
a legislative measure contrary to the constitution is
not law and never was. The alleged explanation
totally ignores the crucial question, which is, *Why is
it the judicial view of the constitution that legislative
measures have to conform to?* The article on the
Dred Scott Decision treats of the most dramatic epi-
sode in the history of judicial review, though one that
is by no means the best illustrative of the spirit of the
institution. The study entitled "We, the People," ap-
proaches the time-honored controversy over Secession
and Nullification from what is shown to be, I submit,

the point of view of 1787.   But the verdict arrived
at with reference to the rights of the States in relation to the Constitution is not without import for some
present-day issues, as is shown in the paper on Some
Possibilities of Treaty-Making.   The paper on the
Pelatiah Webster Myth deals with a question of less
practical significance, but yet one of real ethical importance.   For if history has any function to perform
it is that of endeavoring at least to make correct assess-
ment of the motives and services of men.

In the preparation of this little volume I have become the debtor of Professor Evans Holbrook, editor
of the Michigan Law Review, for valuable editorial assistance in putting the first study into final shape.   My
especial thanks are also due to Mr. Walter Cottrell of
the Princeton University Library staff and Mr. B. A.
Finney of the University of Michigan Library for
numberless courtesies.

I should also take this occasion to point out to the
reader that when the word "constitution" is capi-
talized in the following pages it refers to the national
Constitution, but that at other times it refers to this
or that State constitution or signifies constitution in
the generic sense.   The distinction becomes at times of
some importance.

EDWARD S. CORWIN.

Ypsilanti, Michigan
    Sept. 11, 1914

CONTENTS

vii

MARBURY v. MADISON AND THE DOCTRINE OF JUDICIAL REVIEW

MARBURY v. MADISON AND THE DOCTRINE OF JUDICIAL REVIEW*

What is the *exact legal basis* of the power of the Supreme Court to pass upon the constitutionality of acts of Congress? Recent literature on the subject reveals a considerable variety of opinion. There are radicals who hold that the power owes its existence to an act of sheer usurpation by the Supreme Court itself, in the decision of *Marbury* v. *Madison*.[1] There

* The principal historical studies on this subject are the following: W. M. Meigs, The Relation of the Judiciary to the Constitution, 19 Am. Law Rev. 175-203 (1885); C. B. Elliott, The Legislatures and the Courts, 5 Pol. Sc. Qtly. 224-58 (1890); Brinton Coxe, Judicial Power and Unconstitutional Legislation (Phila., 1893); J. B. Thayer, The American Doctrine of Constitutional Law, 7 Harv. Law Rev. 129-56 (1894); E. S. Corwin, The Rise and Establishment of Judicial Review, 9 Mich. Law Rev. 102-25, 284-316 (1910-11); C. A. Beard, The Supreme Court and the Constitution (N. Y. 1912); J. H. Dougherty, Power of the Federal Judiciary over Legislation (N. Y., 1912); A. C. McLaughlin, The Courts, the Constitution, and Parties (Chicago, 1912); C. H. Burr, Unconstitutional Law and the Federal Judicial Power, 60 Univ. of Pa. Law Rev. and Am. Law Reg. 624-43 (1912); H. Pope, The Fundamental Law and the Courts, 27 Harv. Law Rev. 45-67 (1913); H. A. Davis, Annulment of Legislation by the Supreme Court, 7 Am. Pol. Sc. Rev. 541-87 (1913); C. G. Haines, The Am. Doctrine of Judicial Supremacy (N. Y., 1914); F. E. Melvin, The Judicial Bulwark of the Constitution, 8 Am. Pol. Sc. Rev. 167-203 (1914).

[1] See for example, H. L. Boudin in 26 Pol. Sc. Qtly. 238, or J. B. McDonough, Usurpation of Power by Federal Courts, 46 Am. Law Rev. 45.

I

are conservatives who point to clauses of the Constitution which, they assure us, specifically confer the power.[2]   There are legal writers who refuse to go back of *Marbury* v. *Madison,* content in the ratification which, they assert, subsequent events have given the doctrine of that decision.[3]   There are historical writers who show that a considerable portion of the membership of the body that framed the Constitution are on record as having personally favored judicial review at one time or another, either before, during, or after the Convention.[4]   Finally, there are other historical writers who represent judicial review as the natural outgrowth of ideas that were common property in the period when the Constitution was established.[5]   Both these last views I find to be in themselves correct enough, but with the result of disclosing some more fundamental problems.   For the question is not, what did the framers of the Constitution *hope* or *desire* with reference to judicial review, but what did they *do* with reference to it; and before ideas contemporary with the framing of the Constitution can be regarded as furnishing the *legal* basis of judicial review, it must be shown that they were, by contemporary understand-

[2] Brinton Coxe and J. H. Dougherty, above.

[3] This seems to be the position, for example, of Prof. James Parker Hall, in his Constitutional Law and of Mr. Cotton in his Introduction to his Decisions of John Marshall.

[4] Meigs, Elliott, Beard, Burr, Melvin, above.   Mr. Melvin's researches into this subject are the most thorough.   His article is also valuable for the account it gives of the growth in the Convention of the articles of the Constitution touching judicial power.

[5] The present writer in above cited articles and McLaughlin, The Courts, etc.

ing, incorporated in the Constitution for that purpose
and that they were *logically sufficient* for it.   To in-
vestigate these questions is the purpose of the study
to follow.

I

The position of those who are content to rest the
power of the Supreme Court over acts of Congress
upon *Marbury* v. *Madison*[6] is plainly illogical.   For
either that decision was based upon the Constitution
or it was not.   In the former case, however, it is the
Constitution that is the real basis of the power, while
in the latter the decision was erroneous by the court's
own premises.   Still it is urged that whatever the
defects of the original decision, these have long since
been cured by popular acquiescence and later decisions.
Let me then begin this article by showing some difficulties in the way of this view.

The case of *Marbury* v. *Madison* arose upon an application by plaintiff to the Supreme Court for a writ
of mandamus to the Secretary of State to compel him
to deliver a commission authorizing plaintiff to exercise the functions of an office to which he had been
duly appointed.   The court, reversing the usual order
of procedure,[6a] went first into the merits of the ques-

---

[6] I Cr. 137 (1803).

[6a] "As the first question which this motion presents is one
of the jurisdiction and power of this court to grant the writ
prayed for in this case, it will be following the rule established to consider it first; a rule which ought never to be disregarded where a question of power arises": J. Baldwin in
5 Pet. 190, 200, citing I Cr. 91, 3 Cr. 172, 5 Cr. 221, 9 Wheat.
816, 10 Wheat. 20.

tion and from its review of these came to the conclusion that a mandamus, had it been sought in a tribunal having jurisdiction of the case, would undoubtedly have been the proper remedy. But this, it contended, had not been done. For though § 13 of the Act of 1789 purported to authorize the Supreme Court to issue "writs of mandamus in cases warranted by the principles and usages of law to . . . persons holding office under the authority of the United States,"[7] this provision transgressed Article III, § 2, par. 2, of the Constitution, the words of which describing the original jurisdiction of the Supreme Court must be interpreted as negativing any further power of the same order. Thereupon the court pronounced §13 null and void, and dismissed the case for want of jurisdiction.

Inevitably, the first question raised by Marshall's decision is as to the correctness of his construction of Article III, § 2, par. 2. In support of his position the Chief Justice might have quoted, had he chosen, the Federalist,[8] but against him were: first, the important evidence of the legislative provision overturned, showing congressional opinion practically contemporaneous with the Constitution; secondly, the fact that anterior to *Marbury* v. *Madison* the court itself had repeatedly taken jurisdiction of cases brought under that provision;[9] and thirdly, the fact that in other connections affirmative words of grant

[7] For the Act of 1789, see 1 Statutes at Large 85 ffg. (24 Sept. 1789, c. 20).

[8] Federalist No. 81 (Lodge's Ed., p. 507).

[9] See argument of counsel in 1 Cr. 137-53.

in the Constitution had not been deemed to infer a
correlative negative. Thus, were the rule laid down
in *Marbury* v. *Madison* to be followed, Congress
would have power to enact penalties against only the
crimes of counterfeiting, treason, and piracy and of-
fences against the Law of Nations, whereas in fact
it had, even as early as 1790, enacted penalties against
many other acts, by virtue of its general authority
under the "necessary and proper" clause.[10]

Yet it must be admitted that the rule of exclusive-
ness does often apply to cases of affirmative enumer-
ation, so that the only question is whether Article III,
§ 2, par. 2, furnished such a case. Speaking to this
point, the Chief Justice said: "A negative or exclusive sense must be given them [the words of the
paragraph in question] or they have no operation at
all."[11] But this is simply not so. For though given
only their affirmative value, these words still place the
cases enumerated by them beyond the reach of Congress,—surely no negligible matter. Nor does the
Chief Justice's attempt to draw support from the further words of the same paragraph fare better upon
investigation. "In all other cases," he quotes, the
Supreme Court is given appellate jurisdiction, that is,
as he would have it, *merely* appellate jurisdiction.
Unfortunately for this argument the words thus
pointed to are followed by the words—which the
Chief Justice fails to quote—"with such exceptions
. . . as the Congress shall make." Why, then, should
not the exceptions thus allowed to the appellate juris-

[10] 1 Stat. L. 112 ffg. (Apr. 30, 1790).
[11] 1 Cr. 174.

diction of the Supreme Court have been intended to take the form, if Congress so willed, of giving the court original jurisdiction of the cases covered by them?

Moreover, the time was to come when Marshall himself was to abandon the reasoning underlying the rule laid down in *Marbury* v. *Madison*. This rule, to repeat, was that the Supreme Court's original jurisdiction is confined by the Constitution to the cases specifically enumerated in Article III, § 2, par. 2, and—though this was only dictum—that the court's appellate jurisdiction is confined "to all other cases." But now it must be noted that jurisdiction is always *either original or appellate,*—that there is, in other words, no third sort. The rule laid down in *Marbury* v. *Madison* becomes therefore the logical equivalent of the proposition that the Supreme Court had *only* original jurisdiction of the cases enumerated in Article III, § 2, par. 2. In *Cohens* v. *Virginia*[12] nevertheless the court took jurisdiction on appeal of a case which had arisen "under this Constitution," but was also a case to which a State was party, on the basis of the rule, as stated by the Chief Justice, that "Where the words admit of appellate jurisdiction the power to take cognizance of the suit originally does not necessarily negative the power to decide upon it on an appeal, if it may originate in a different court."[13] And in further illustration of this rule, the Chief Justice instanced the right of the Supreme Court to take jurisdiction on appeal of certain cases which foreign

[12] 6 Wheat. 264 (1821).
[13] *Ib.* 395-402.

consuls were allowed to institute in the lower federal courts.[14] He also insisted, and quite warrantably, upon the necessity of the rule in question to major purposes of the Constitution. Yet obviously if the rule is to be harmonized with that laid down in *Marbury* v. *Madison,* it must be by eliminating the word "all" from the opening clause of Article III, § 2, par. 2, and by inserting qualifying words in front of the word "those" of the same clause. Otherwise the line of reasoning taken in *Marbury* v. *Madison* is abandoned and the precise decision there left hanging in mid-air.[15]

Suppose however, we concede Marshall his construction of Article III, is his decision absolved of error thereby? By no means. This decision rests upon the assumption that it was the intention and necessary operation of § 13 of the Act of 1789 to *enlarge* the original jurisdiction of the Supreme Court, and this cannot be allowed. To begin with, in Common Law practice, in the light of which § 13 was framed, the writ of mandamus was not, ordinarily at least, an instrument of obtaining jurisdiction by a court, even upon appeal, but like the writs of habeas corpus and injunction, was a *remedy* available from a

[14] The validity of such appeals was considered by C. J. Taney in *Gittings* v. *Crawford,* Federal Cases, 5,465. Referring to the precise clause, under discussion in *Marbury* v. *Madison,* Taney said: "In the clause in question there is nothing but mere affirmative words of grant, and none that import a design to exclude the subordinate jurisdiction of other courts of the United States on the same subject-matter." See also C. J. Waite's language in *Ames* v. *Kansas,* 111 U. S. 449.

[15] The precise precedent in *Marbury* v. *Madison* has been applied several times. See 5 How. 176, 1 Wall. 243, 8 Wall. 85.

court in the exercise of its standing jurisdiction. This being the case, however, why may it not have been the intention of Congress in enacting § 13, not to enlarge the Supreme Court's jurisdiction, but simply to enable the court to issue the writ of mandamus to civil officers of the United States as auxiliary to the original jurisdiction which the Constitution conferred upon it? It is certain that the court has more than once entertained motions by original suitors for injunctions to such officers,[16] and it is apparent that, so far as the question here discussed is concerned, an application for a writ of mandamus must rest on the same footing.[17]

Furthermore, the proposition that the writ of mandamus is not to be regarded ordinarily as a means of obtaining jurisdiction, but only of exercising it, was recognized and applied by the Supreme Court itself a few years later, in a case the exact parallel of *Marbury* v. *Madison*. By § 14 of the Act of 1789 the circuit courts of the United States were given the power, in words substantially the same as those employed in § 13, to issue certain writs "in cases authorized by the principles and usages of law." Yet in *McIntire* v. *Wood*,[18] where the issue was the validity of a writ of mandamus to a person holding office

---

[16] *Miss.* v. *Johnson*, 4 Wall. 475; *Ga.* v. *Stanton*, 6 Wall. 50. The grounds on which these cases were dismissed do not affect the view urged in the text.

[17] Suppose Congress should transfer the business of interstate extradition to federal commissioners, as it would be within its power to do, there would be plenty of occasions when the Supreme Court would be asked for writs of mandamus to civil officers of the United States. See *Ky.* v. *Dennison*, 24 How. 65.

[18] 7 Cr. 504 (1813).

under the authority of the United States the Supreme
Court ruled that before a circuit court could utilize
the power given it in § 14 in a case, it must have
jurisdiction of the case on independent grounds, and
the same rule was later reiterated in *McClung* v. *Silli-
man*.[19] But clearly, had the court followed this line
of reasoning in *Marbury* v. *Madison,* it could not have
questioned the validity of § 13. Indeed, had it but
followed the, today at any rate, well-known maxim of
Constitutional Law that of two possible interpretations of a statute, the one harmonious with the Constitution, the other at variance with it, the former
must be preferred,[20] it could not have challenged the
legislation in question. By its view of Article III,
§ 2, par. 2, it must still doubtless have declined jurisdiction of the case, but the ground of its action would
have been, not the error of Congress, but the error of
plaintiff.

In short there was no valid occasion in *Marbury* v.
Madison for any inquiry by the court into its prerogative in relation to acts of Congress. Why then, it
will be asked, did the court make such an inquiry?
In part the answer to this question will appear later,
but in part it may be answered now. To speak quite
frankly, this decision bears many of the earmarks of
a deliberate partisan *coup*. The court was bent on
reading the President a lecture on his legal and moral
duty to recent Federalist appointees to judicial office,
whose commissions the last Administration had not

[19] 6 Wheat. 598 (1821).
[20] For a rather far-fetched application of this rule see the
"Commodities Clause" Case, 213 U. S. 366 (1908).

had time to deliver, but at the same time hesitated to invite a snub by actually asserting jurisdiction of the matter. It therefore took the engaging position of declining to exercise power which the Constitution withheld from it, by making the occasion an opportunity to assert a far more transcendent power.

II

But from *Marbury* v. *Madison* we proceed to the question whether, and in what way, the Constitution itself sanctions judicial review. I have already indicated my opinion that no clause was inserted in the Constitution for the specific purpose of bestowing this power on courts, but that the power rests upon certain general principles thought by its framers to have been embodied in the Constitution. I shall now endeavor to justify this opinion.

That the members of the Convention of 1787 thought the Constitution secured to courts in the United States the right to pass on the validity of acts of Congress under it cannot be reasonably doubted. Confining ourselves simply to the available evidence that is strictly contemporaneous with the framing and ratifying of the Constitution, as I think it only proper to do, we find the following members of the Convention that framed the Constitution definitely asserting that this would be the case: Gerry and King of Massachusetts, Wilson and Gouverneur Morris of Pennsylvania, Martin of Maryland, Randolph, Madison, and Mason of Virginia, Dickinson of Delaware, Yates and Hamilton of New York, Rutledge and Charles Pinckney of South Carolina, Davie and Williamson of North Carolina, Sherman and Ellsworth of Connecticut.[21] True these are only seventeen names out of a possible fifty-five, but let it be considered whose names they are. They designate fully three-fourths of the leaders of the Convention, four of the five members of the Committee of Detail which drafted the Constitution,[22] and four of the five members of the Committee of Style which gave the Constitution final form.[23] The entries under these names, in the Index to Farrand's Records occupy fully thirty columns, as compared with fewer than half as many

[21] Max Farrand, Records of the Federal Convention (Yale Univ. Press, 1913) ; I, 97 (Gerry), 109 (King) ; II, 73 (Wilson), 76 (Martin), 78 (Mason), 299 (Dickinson and Morris), 428 (Rutledge), 248 (Pinckney), 376 (Williamson), 28 (Sherman, 93 (Madison) ; III, 220 (Martin, in "Genuine Information"). The Federalist: Nos. 39 and 44 (Madison), No. 78 (Hamilton). Elliot's Debates (Ed. of 1836) ; II, 1898-9 (Ellsworth), 417 and 454 (Wilson), 336-7 (Hamilton) ; III, 197, 208, 431 (Randolph), 441 (Mason), 484-5 (Madison) ; IV, 165 (Davie). P. L. Ford, Pamphlets on the Constitution, 184 (Dickinson, in "Letters of Fabius"). Ford, Essays on the Constitution, 295 (Yates, writing as "Brutus"). Pinckney later, in 1799, denounced the idea of judicial review, thus: "On no subject am I more convinced than that it is an unsafe and dangerous doctrine in a republic ever to suppose that a judge ought to possess the right of questioning or deciding upon the constitutionality of treaties, laws, or any act of the legislature. It is placing the opinion of an individual, or two, or three, above that of both branches of Congress, a doctrine which is not warranted by the Constitution, and will not, I hope, long have any advocates in this country"; quoted from Wharton's State Trials, 412, by Mr. Horace A. Davis in Am. Polit. Sc. Rev., 551. Madison's later views are considered *infra*.

[22] Gorham, Rutledge, Randolph, Ellsworth, and Wilson. The argument is from Professor Beard's Supreme Court, etc.

[23] Johnson, Hamilton, Morris, Madison, and King.

columns under the names of the remaining members.
We have in this list, in other words, the names of men
who expressed themselves on the subject of judicial
review because they also expressed themselves on all
other subjects before the Convention. They were the
leaders of that body and its articulate members. And
against them are to be pitted, in reference to the question under discussion, only Mercer of Maryland, Bedford of Delaware, and Spaight of North Carolina, the
record in each of whose cases turns out to be upon
inspection of doubtful implication. For while
Spaight, for instance, undoubtedly expressed himself,
during the period of the Convention, as strongly adverse to the theory of judicial review,[24] yet he later
heard the idea expounded both on the floor of the
Philadelphia Convention and the North Carolina convention without protest. The words of Bedford which
are relied upon in this connection are his declaration
that he was "opposed to every check on the legislature." But these words were spoken with reference,
not to judicial review, but to the proposition to establish a council of legislative revision.[25] Mercer of
Maryland did not sign the Constitution and opposed
its adoption. It is by no means impossible that one of
the grounds of his opposition was recognition of the
fact that the Constitution established judicial review.[26]
Altogether it seems a warrantable assertion that on
no other feature of the Constitution with reference

[24] See McRee, Life and Correspondence of James Iredell, II,
169-76.
[25] Farrand, I, 100, 106.
[26] Ib. II, 298.

to which there has been any considerable debate is the view of the Convention itself better attested.

Yet it must be admitted that, if we assume that the Convention did not finally incorporate its view in specific provisions of the Constitution, a difficulty that at first seems formidable opposes itself to the thesis that this view was secured by certain general principles thought to be embodied in the Constitution. The source of the difficulty I allude to is Article VI, par. 2, of the Constitution. This paragraph first announces the *supremacy* of the Constitution, the acts of Congress in pursuance thereof, and treaties made under the authority of the United States, as *law* of the land, and then proceeds to impose a specific mandate upon *State* judges to enforce this *supreme law,* anything in the law or constitution of any State to the contrary notwithstanding. The question therefore arises, Why did the Convention, if it believed general principles sufficient to secure judicial review of acts of Congress, deem it necessary to order the *State* judges to prefer what was described as *supreme* law of the land to subordinate law? Any doctrine of judicial review must rest in part upon the idea of one law superior to another, and if, to repeat the question just put, the fact of superiority of national law to State law furnished, in the estimation of the Convention, an insufficient security of the former as against the latter, why should not the analogous superiority of the Constitution itself to acts of Congress be similarly insufficient? But the answer to this question is, after all, plain enough: The judges to whom the mandate of Article VI is addressed are *State* judges, that is, judges of an independent jurisdiction. Their duty to take cognizance of national law *at all* had therefore to be declared in unmistakable terms. Indeed, once this fact is grasped, it is seen that the mandate in question, instead of opposing difficulty to the thesis I am presenting, furnishes it powerful confirmation. For the significant feature of that mandate now becomes the fact that it is addressed to State *judges,* who are thus assumed to be the *final* guardians of both State laws and State *constitutions.*

What, however, are the clauses usually represented as having been placed in the Constitution for the purpose of giving the Supreme Court the power to pass upon the validity of acts of Congress? One is the "pursuance" clause of Article VI, par. 2. But obviously this clause, while perhaps making more explicit the fact that Congress' is a limited power, says nothing as to what agency is to say *finally* what of Congress' acts are, and what are not, "in pursuance of this Constitution." Moreover, the "pursuance" clause does not appear in Article III, which deals with the judicial power of the United States.

A clause more insisted upon, however, in this connection is the clause in this same Article III: "The judicial power of the United States shall extend to all cases arising under this Constitution." No doubt it must be allowed that cases involving the question of constitutionality with reference to acts of Congress are describable as "cases arising under this Constitution." Nevertheless, it must be insisted that the clause just quoted was not placed in the Constitution for the purpose of bringing such cases within the judicial

power of the United States, and this for the simple
reason that they were already there. As we have just
noted, the "pursuance" clause does not appear in
Article III. But what this signifies is that the judicial
power of the United States extends to *every* act of
Congress whether made in pursuance of the Constitution or not, that—to quote the words of Chief Justice
Taney in *Ableman* v. *Booth*—it "covers every legislative act of Congress, whether it be made within the
limits of its delegated power or be an assumption of
power beyond the grants in the Constitution."[27] Had,
therefore, the clause "arising under this Constitution"
been inserted to extend the judicial power of the
United States to cases involving the constitutionality
of acts of Congress, it would be so far forth mere
surplusage.

The explanation of the clause must then be sought
in a class of cases to which *but for it* the judicial
power of the United States would not extend. Nor,
relying upon the guidance of Hamilton in the Federalist is it difficult to discover such a class of cases.
Construing the clause under discussion in Federalist
80, Hamilton explains that it refers to cases arising in
consequence of *State* enactments transgressing prohibitions of the Constitution upon *State* legislative
powers, cases which, therefore, but for this clause,
would terminate in the *State* judiciaries. Hamilton's
explanation is confirmed by Madison's analysis of
Article III in the Virginia convention[28] and by Davie's
language in the North Carolina convention.[29]

[27] 21 How. 506, 519-20 (1858).
[28] Elliot, III, 484-5.
[29] *Ib.* IV, 165.

But a more vital consideration is that the "arising" clause does not, *unless we take a certain view of the Constitution and of judicial power under it,* confer upon the federal courts the power to pass *finally* upon the validity of even State laws under the Constitution,—*finally, that is, as against Congress,* which has the power to pass all laws "necessary and proper" to carry its enumerated powers into effect and whose laws passed by warrant of this power are paramount to all conflicting State laws or constitutions.[29a]   The purpose of the clause is merely to define the jurisdiction of the federal courts.   The "judicial power" of the United States, it says, shall extend to certain classes of "cases."   But as to *what* that power is, what are its intrinsic nature and scope, it says not a word.

Nor is the list of objections yet exhausted to resting the power of the Supreme Court over acts of Congress upon the phrases under discussion.   For one thing, it may be asked, if these phrases are necessary to give the federal courts power to pass upon the constitutionality of acts of Congress, what becomes of the similar pretension of State courts with reference to State legislation under the State constitutions, from which these or equivalent phrases are usually absent? Again, it may be asked, how, upon this assumption, is the fact to be explained that most of the advocates of judicial review in the Convention of 1787 had declared their belief that this power would reside in the national courts long before they had heard or thought of these clauses?   Finally, it may be asked why, if the framers wanted judicial review and still thought

[29a] See particularly Fed. 33 (Lodge's Ed.).

it necessary to provide for it specifically, did they not choose language apt for the purpose, language as explicit and unmistakable as that describing, for example, the veto power of the President? A possible answer would be, of course, that they desired to conceal their intentions at this point, but the fact is, that they proclaimed them and that judicial review was universally regarded as a feature of the new system while its adoption was pending.[30]

III

In short, we are driven to the conclusion that judicial review was rested by the framers of the Constitution upon certain general principles which in their estimation made specific provision for it unnecessary, in the same way as, for example, certain other general principles made unnecessary specific provision for the President's power of removal.[31] What, then, are these general principles? The task of identifying them is, perhaps, at this date not an entirely simple one. For while the ideas that are essential to explaining and sustaining judicial review *as a matter of law,* which are the ideas we are in quest of, are relatively few, they have to be sifted from a more considerable stock of ideas which contributed to the rise of judicial review, *as a matter of fact,* or which have since been offered with the aim of curtailing its practical operation. It will be profitable to begin by

[30] See note at the end of this article, on Judicial Review in the Ratifying Conventions.

[31] The parallel is exact. See Annals of Congress, I, cols. 473 ffg. and especially cols. 481-2.

criticising some remarks of Professor McLaughlin, made in the course of his recent interesting study of the subject.

At the outset of his essay, writing with Marshall's argument in *Marbury* v. *Madison* in mind, Professor McLaughlin states the doctrine of judicial review as follows: "In theory any court may exercise the power of holding acts invalid; in doing so, it assumes no special and peculiar role; for the duty of the court is to declare what the law is, and, on the other hand, not to recognize and apply what is not law." Further along, however, he sets himself the task of refuting the idea that the courts claim a superiority over the other departments in relation to the constitution, and we then find him writing thus: "This authority then in part arose . . . from the conviction that the courts were not under the control of a coördinate branch of the government but entirely able to interpret the constitution themselves when acting in their own field." And from this it is quite logically deduced that, "If our constitutional system at the present time includes the principle that the political departments must yield to the decisions of the judiciary on the whole question of constitutionality, such principle is the result of constitutional development, and . . . of the acquiescence of the political powers, because of reasons of expediency." Yet at the same time it is conceded that the political departments must "accept as final" "the decision of the court in the particular case." Finally, it is urged that "no one is bound by an unconstitutional law."[32]

[32] The Courts, the Constitution, and Parties, pp. 6, 51, 55, 56.

In other words, Professor McLaughlin presents the
right of interpreting the constitution that is enjoyed
by the courts, first, as a *judicial* power, and therefore
one to be exercised by courts *as such;* secondly, as a
departmental or official function, and therefore one
to be exercised by all departments of government
equally, *including the courts;* and thirdly, as an individual prerogative, and therefore one belonging to
everybody, *including judges.* In the first place, there
is an element of inconsistency among these three
theories that should not escape our attention. For if
the power of the judiciary to construe the constitution, when acting in its own field, owes anything by
way of *theoretical justification*—which is the point
under discussion—to its position as an independent
branch of the government, why is it necessary to insist
on the legal character of the constitution and the
duty of courts to interpret the law? Likewise, if the
position of the judiciary as an equal and coördinate
branch of the government, or of judges as governmental functionaries, is an indispensible foundation
of judicial review, why is it necessary to contend that
"no one is bound by an unconstitutional act"?

But a more important criticism is that the two last
theories are either quite unallowable or totally insufficient to explain judicial review. Let us consider,
first, the statement that "no one is bound by an unconstitutional law." This may mean one of two
things: either that no one is bound by a law that has
been determined by proper authority to be unconstitutional, which leaves open the crucial question as to

where this proper authority resides; or, that no one is bound by a law which *he* thinks is unconstitutional, which is nonsense. It is not open to contradiction that judicial review posits a constitutional system, complete in all points, and furnished with the machinery for determining all questions that arise out of it. But the right of revolution is a right external to any constitution, and therefore to invoke it as a means of settling constitutional questions is to discard the constitution at the outset.[33]

And similarly is the doctrine that the power to construe the constitution is a departmental function allowable or unallowable according as one understands it. If what is meant by it is that all functionaries of government have to interpret the constitution prelimi-

[33] Vattel's Apothegm that the legislature cannot "change the constitution without destroying the foundation of its authority" was a commonplace in Massachusetts before the Revolution: see the Massachusetts Circular Letter of 1768 in MacDonald, Documentary Source Book, 146-50. For interesting statements basing judicial review on the right of revolution, see Elliot, II, 100-06 (Parsons in the Massachusetts convention), and IV, 93-4 (Steele in the North Carolina convention); also note 58, below. In confirmation of the view set forth in the text, that judicial review is not a revolutionary function, are the following words by Curtis, Const'l Hist. II, 13 (Ed. of 1890): "The government of the U. S. has no prerogative which entitles it to be exempt from revolution, when the people choose to resort to that desperate remedy. It must defend its rightful existence and authority by the means with which the Constitution has clothed it. But the right to resort to revolution against intolerable oppression is governed by no law. The right to find relief against an act of Congress which transcends its constitutional powers springs from and is regulated by the Constitution itself. It is a right that can be exercised only by resorting to a judicial remedy."

nary to performing their supposed duties under it, in the same way that the private citizen has to interpret the ordinary law whenever he performs an act having legal consequences—why the theory is correct enough, but perhaps hardly necessary. On the other hand, if what is meant is that the three departments have an equal right, when acting within their respective spheres, to determine the validity of their own acts, then it is untrue.

But the second meaning is in fact, as we shall see later, the meaning which was attached to the doctrine by those who brought it forth, *not to support judicial review but to arrest it.* And this is still its meaning in the classic statement of it in President Jackson's famous Veto Message of July 10, 1832. Said the President on that occasion:

"The Congress, the Executive, and the Court must each for itself be guided by its own opinion of the Constitution. Each public officer who takes an oath to support the Constitution swears that he will support it as he understands it, and not as it is understood by others. . . . The opinion of the judges has no more authority over Congress than the opinion of Congress has over the judges; and, on that point, the President is independent of both."[34]

The day following the appearance of the message, Webster replied to it, on the floor of the Senate, in the following terms:

"The President is as much bound by the law as any private citizen. . . . He may refuse to obey the law and so may any private citizen, but both do it at their own peril and neither can settle the question of its validity.

[34] J. D. Richardson, Messages and Papers of the Presidents, II, 582.

The President may *say* a law is unconstitutional, but he is not the judge. . . . If it were otherwise, there would be not government of laws, but we should all live under the government, the rule, the caprices of individuals; . . . The President, if the principle and reasoning of the message be sound, may either execute or not execute the laws of the land, according to his sovereign pleasure. He may refuse to put into execution one law, pronounced valid by all branches of government, and yet execute another which may have been by constitutional authority pronounced void." The message converted "constitutional limitations of power into mere matters of opinion," denied "first principles," contradicted "truths heretofore received as indisputable," *denied "to the judiciary the interpretation of the law."*

And Webster elsewhere inquired, with pertinent reference to a then impending issue: "Does nullification teach anything more revolutionary?"[35]

But indeed, Professor McLaughlin too urges that the political departments are obliged "to accept as final . . . the decision of the court in the particular case." Yet he also contends that further acquiescence by these departments in the views of the judiciary on constitutional questions is not required by constitutional theory, but must be reckoned as "accommodation" on their part based on reasons of expediency. The significance of this view all hinges on the meaning of the word "decision" in the phrase "decision of the court in the particular case." This may mean

[35] Speech of July 11, 1832; speech of Oct. 12, 1832, before the Whig convention at Worcester, Mass.: Works, II, 122 (National Ed.). The logical implications of Jackson's doctrine were soon illustrated. At the close of this year the Sup. Ct. rendered its decision in *Worcester* v. *Ga.*, 6 Pet. 515, which the Pres. refused to enforce, saying: "John Marshall has made his decision, now let him enforce it": Greeley, Am. Conflict, I, 106.

merely the *judgment* of the court on the question of rights at issue between the parties to the case or it may mean, where the judgment is based on the nullity of an act of the legislature, the court's determination that the act was null, or, even more broadly, the reasons given by the court for this determination. To discuss the last meaning would take us too far afield, and is unnecessary. For even if we take the second meaning as the correct one, the right of the court to pass *finally* on the validity of the acts of the legislature as these come before it is admitted, and the doctrine of departmental construction of the constitution is *quoad hoc* abandoned.

But it may have been Professor McLaughlin's intention to voice acceptance of a theory which has the support of Bancroft, Meigs, and other authorities, and which, stated in its clearest form, runs thus:

"The judicial power extends to the determination of 'cases,' not questions. . . . There is no power in the courts to annul an act of Congress, but only to decide cases'. . . . There is no power anywhere to annul an act because deemed unconstitutional. The President may declare that, in his opinion, an act is void because unconstitutional, and refuse to enforce it; and so may the courts; but neither can control the other. . . . The judiciary can no more annul an act of Congress on the ground of its unconstitutionality than Congress can set aside a decree of the courts because without jurisdiction."[36]

[36] R. G. Street, 6 Reports of Am. Bar Assoc., 184-6. Bancroft's view is to be found on page 350 of volume VI of his History (Last Revision), thus: "The decision of the court in all cases within its jurisdiction is final between the parties to a suit and must be carried into effect by the proper officers; but as an interpretation of the Constitution, it does not bind the

Obviously the question raised by this theory is as to the correctness of the view it states of the scope of judicial duty. The courts, it is said, decide cases, and it is thence concluded that the other departments must support them in the exercise of their constitutional prerogative. This definition of the scope of judicial duty is, however, erroneous. It is not the duty nor yet the power of courts to *decide* cases, but to decide them *in accordance with the law,* of which the constitution is part and parcel; and if the other departments are bound by their decisions it is because they are *presumed* by the constitution itself to be in accordance with the constitution and laws. Otherwise, we should be confronted with the solecism of those sworn to support the constitution obliged by it to promote its violation on occasion. The courts then must ascertain the meaning of the constitution and laws, from which it would seem to follow that those who are bound by the constitution are bound by the judicial view of it in the same general sense as that in which those bound by the ordinary law are bound by the judicial view of *it.* In neither case does the judicial view attempt to constrain *opinion* but it does set the standard of *acts* when these fall within judicial cognizance.

But not only does the theory under discussion land us in paradox, but it is contrary to fact. The *fact* of the matter is that the courts *do* annul legislative acts,

President or the Legislature of the United States." This view is stated *ex cathedra* and without any attempt at argument, and three pages later (p. 353) is substantially contradicted. Mr. Meig's view will be found in 19 Am. Law Rev. 190-203.

in the sense of pronouncing *void* those which *they* think to be contrary to the constitution, and the further *fact* is that they *must* do so if they are not to enforce those acts in particular cases. The matter most sharply and immediately before the court in a case involving the constitutional question is the fact that the constitution endows the legislature with the power to make laws in harmony with it,[37] which means however, not merely the power of putting projects of legislation through the proper parliamentary stages, but *also that of vesting them with the force and sanction of law.*[37a] Unless, therefore, the court is to assume to deprive the legislature of its right in this respect, it must either always assume the will of the legislature to be accordant with the constitution or it must be able to plead its own constitutional right to pronounce on the validity of the acts of the legislature under the constitution,—and there is no third way about the matter. It is true, of

[37] Hence the rule that an act of the legislature must be annulled only when *clearly* unconstitutional, that is, the court must not run the risk of violating the Constitution itself, which it would do if it deprived the legislature of power. In this connection, consider the language of C. J. Richardson in *Dartmouth College* v. *Woodward,* 1 N. H. 111, 115 (1817): "If we refuse to execute an act warranted by the constitution, our decision in effect alters that instrument and imposes new restraints upon the legislative power which the people never intended."

[37a] In this connection note the doctrine that the legislature cannot delegate its power, which signifies in relation to referendum measures (save in connection with local government), that it cannot submit to the voters the question whether a legislative measure shall be *operative or not.* See Cooley, Const'l Lims., (7th Ed.) 168 ffg.

course, that the court does not order the legislature arrested for trying to violate the constitution, but neither does it order a man arrested for trying to make a contract contrary to the statute of frauds or a will contrary to the rule against perpetuities. The penalty which the legislature and the man suffer in such cases is the same,—they have their acts disallowed by the court.

And thus much for a controversy which, first and last, has consumed a good deal of paper, ink, and dialectical skill, and which, not unlikely, will continue its ravages on these commodities. The matrix of the quarrel seems to have been a wrong view of the proper scope and efficacy of the idea of three co-ordinate departments. This idea is well enough in its place, which is to fortify each department in the proper use of its powers, but it throws no light whatever upon the question as to what those powers are, and still less, if possible, does it warrant the claim "that any department can properly exercise any power committed to another."[38]

It is accordingly submitted that judicial review rests upon the following propositions and can rest upon no others: 1—That the constitution binds the organs of government; 2—That it is law in the sense of being known to and enforceable by the courts; 3—That the function of interpreting the standing law appertains to the courts alone, so that their interpretations of the constitution as part and parcel of such standing law

[38] C. C. Bonney, 6 Am. Bar Assoc. Reps., 16. See further the Note at the end of this article on the Doctrine of Departmental Construction.

are, in all cases coming within judicial cognizance, alone authoritative, while those of the other departments are mere expressions of opinion. That the framers of the Constitution of the United States accepted the first of these propositions goes without saying. Their acceptance of the second one is registered in the Constitution itself, though this needs to be shown. But it is their acceptance of the third one which is the matter of greatest significance, for at this point their view marks an entire breach, not only with English legal tradition, but, for the vast part, with American legal tradition as well, anterior to 1787.

IV

The idea of judicial review is today regarded as an outgrowth of that of a written constitution, but historically both are offshoots from a common stock, namely the idea of certain fundamental principles underlying and controlling government. In Anglo-American constitutional history this idea is to be traced to feudal concepts and finds its most notable expression in Magna Carta.[39] The notion was well suited to a period when the great institutions of mankind were thought to be sacred, permanent, immutable, and did in fact alter but slowly. The period of the Reformation, however, was a period of overturn, of defiance of ancient establishments, of revolution. Its precipitate for political theory was the notion, derived

[39] See C. H. McIlwain, The High Court of Parliament and its Supremacy (1911), and G. B. Adams, The Origin of the English Constitution (1912).

from Roman law, of *sovereignty,* of human authority
in the last analysis uncontrollable, and capable accordingly of meeting the exigencies of the new *régime*
of Change.

But where did sovereignty rest? Sir Thomas
Smith, in his Commonwealth of England, reflecting
Tudor ideas, attributed it to the Crown in Parliament,[40] and it is not impossible that English political
theory would have remained from that day to this substantially what it is today but for the attempt of James
Stuart to set up the notion, on the basis of Divine
Right, of a kingly prerogative recognized but uncontrolled by the Common Law. The result was a
reaction headed by Sir Edward Coke and having for
its purpose, in the quaint words of Sir Benjamin
Rudyard, "to make that good old, decrepid law of
Magna Carta, which hath so long been kept in and
bed-ridden, as it were, to walk again."[41] Coke took
the position that there was no such thing as sovereign
power in England, even for Parliament; for, said he:
"Magna Carta is such a fellow that he will have no
sovereign." His famous dictum in *Dr. Bonham's
Case*[42] that an act of Parliament "contrary to common
right and reason" would be "void," was therefore
quite in harmony with his whole propaganda. At the
same time, it would be the height of absurdity to sup-

[40] F. W. Maitland, Constitutional History, 255. Maitland ex-
presses the emphatic opinion that the law-making power of
Crown and Parliament was from an early date unlimited.

[41] Cobbett, Parliamentary History, II, col. 335; the remark
quoted below is from the same debate, col. 357.

[42] 8 Reps. 107, 118 (1612).

pose that these words spell out anything like judicial
review. They undoubtedly indicate Coke's belief that
the principles of "common right and reason," being
part of the Common Law, were cognizable by the
judges while interpreting acts of Parliament. For the
rest, however, they must be read along with Coke's
characterization of Parliament as the *"Supreme
Court"* of the realm. Being a *court,* Parliament was
necessarily bound by the law, even as it declared and
elaborated it; but being the *highest* court, its interpretations of the law necessarily bound all other courts.
As he plainly indicated, both by his *words,* in his Institutes, and *practically,* by his connection with the
framing of the Petition of Right, Coke regarded
Parliament itself as the *final* interpreter of the law
by which both it, the King, and the judges were
bound.[43]

The inaugural event in the history of American
Constitutional Law, however, was the argument made
by James Otis at Boston in February 1761, in the
Writs of Assistance Case. The question at issue was
whether the British customs officials, one Paxton in
particular, should be furnished with general search
warrants enabling them to search for smuggled goods.
The application was opposed for the Boston mer-
chants by Thacher and Otis. Thacher contented himself with denying that such a writ as was asked for
was warranted by any act of Parliament and, more
particularly, that the court to whom the application

---

[43] See note at the end of this article on The True Meaning of
Coke's Dictum.

had been made had authority in the premises. Otis, on the other hand, plunged at once into the most fundamental issues. His argument was, that whether such writs were warranted by act of Parliament or not, was a matter of indifference, since such act of Parliament would be "against the constitution" and "against natural equity" and therefore void. *"If,"* he accordingly concluded, *"an act of Parliament should be made in the very words of this petition, it would be void. The executive courts must pass such acts into disuse."*[44]

Was there then any warrant in law for this conclusion? No. The proposition that an act of Parliament contrary to "common right and reason" was "void" had indeed been repeated *obiter* by Coke's contemporary, Hobart, and later by Holt, and had found its way into some of the abridgments and commentaries,—works which are apt to be more comprehensive than critical,—but with it hitherto had never been joined the proposition that an inferior court might override the will of Parliament *if this were unmistakably expressed.*[45] On the contrary, in *Captain Streater's Case,* in which, in 1653, Otis' argument had been anticipated, the idea had been specifically rejected. "Mr. Streater," said the judge in that case,, "one must be above another and the inferior must submit to the superior, and in all justice an inferior

---

[44] See Quincy, Early Mass. Reps., note to Paxton's Case, pp. 469-85; also, John Adams, Life and Works, II, 521-5.

[45] See note to Paxton's Case, Quincy, pp. 521-30 and notes, with references to Bacon's Abridgment (1735), Viner's Abridgment (1741-51), Comyn's Digest (1762-67). Hobart's dictum

court cannot control what Parliament does. If Parliament should do one thing and we do the contrary here, things would run round. We must submit to the legislative power."[46]

Nevertheless, having been formulated at the moment when Americans were beginning to lay about them for weapons with which to resist the pretensions of Parliament, Otis' doctrine met with a degree of success,—enough at least to make it a permanent memory with the men of the time. Otis himself, it is true, soon abandoned his own offspring, while his reporter John Adams, in arguing a second case involving the question of the right of Parliament to authorize writs of assistance, maintained a significant silence on the doctrine. In Virginia, on the other hand, the supreme court of the colony, having been put the question, early in 1766, whether officers of

occurs in *Savadge* v. *Day*, Hob. 85 (1615); Holt's dictum occurs in *City of London* v. *Wood*, 12 Mod. 669 (1701). "Coke Lyttleton," wrote Jefferson, with reference to the period when he was a law student, "was the universal book of students and a sounder Whig never wrote nor one of profounder learning in the orthodox doctrines of the British Constitution or what is called British rights." Writing in 1759, Cadwallader Colden makes casual references to a "judicial power of declaring them [laws] void": N. Y. Hist'l Soc. Cols. II, 204. In his study on Colonial Common Law, Professor Reinsch refers to the case of *Giddings* v. *Brown* in which a Mass. magistrate (apparently in the 17th century) pronounced a town resolve voting taxes to build the minister a house "against fundamental law," and void: Select Essays in Anglo-Am. Legal Hist., I, 376. For further instances of the influence of the doctrine under discussion, see Chalmers, Political Annals, N. Y. Hist'l Soc. Cols., I, 81; and Chalmers, Colonial Opinions, 373-82.

[46] St. Trials, II, 196 ffg.

the law would incur a penalty if they did not use stamped paper in conformance with the prescriptions of the Stamp Act, answered that that act did not bind the inhabitants of Virginia, "inasmuch as they conceived" it "to be unconstitutional"; while six years later, George Mason, whose argument was reported by Jefferson, contended in behalf of clients that the same doctrine was applicable to the case of local legislation that was "contrary to natural right." And thence the theory returned to its place of origin. On the very eve of the Declaration of Independence, Judge Cushing, later one of the original bench of the Supreme Court of the United States charged a Massachusetts jury to ignore certain acts of Parliament as "void" and "inoperative." It was a true case of "judicial review" by virtue of the right of revolution.[47]

Meanwhile, however, a new element had entered American political thinking,—the notion of *legislative sovereignty,* from the pages of Blackstone. The grand result of this notion was eventually the establishment of the distinction between "natural law," in the broad general sense of the *moral law,* and "civil law" and the confinement of civil obligation in the last analysis to the latter. Blackstone himself is enough of a conservative to treat "natural law," "divine law," and the like, as in some sense "law," but it is not law, he finally admits, potent to control the will of the

[47] The opinion of the Va. judges on the Stamp Act (Feb. 1766) is described by McMaster, Hist., V, 394. Mason's argument in *Robin* v. *Hardaway* is to be found in Jefferson's (Va.) Reps., 109 ffg. Adam's argument in the *Advocate-General* v. *Hancock* is to be found in Quincy, *loc. cit.,* 459-62.

legislature. Considering, therefore, the statement "that acts of Parliament contrary to reason are void," he says:

"But if the Parliament will positively enact a thing to be done which is unreasonable, I know of no power in the ordinary forms of the constitution that is vested with authority to control it; and the examples usually alleged in support of the rule do none of them prove that where the main object of the statute is unreasonable the judges are at liberty to reject it; for, that were to set the judicial power above that of the legislature, which would be subversive of all government."

The only acts of Parliament, accordingly, which the judges could ignore were acts "impossible to be performed."[48]

Strange it is that this exception, which indeed is in the nature of a self-identical proposition, should have furnished the entering wedge for judicial review in this country after the establishment of Independence. Yet such is the fact. The most influential case in which judicial review was broached before the Convention of 1787 was that of *Trevett* v. *Weeden,* in which, in 1786, the Rhode Island judges

[48] Comms. I, 91. "Sovereignty and legislative power are indeed convertible terms; one cannot subsist without the other": *ib.,* 46. According to Chancellor Kent, 2,500 copies of the commentaries had been sold in America before the outbreak of the Revolution. Jefferson testifies that many young lawyers, "seduced by the honeyed Mansfieldism of Blackstone, began to slide into Toryism." But the Patriots themselves felt the influence. Their final position was no longer one of reliance on the "British Constitution" and "fundamental law," but to oppose the claim of the colonial assemblies as local parliaments to that of the imperial Parliament: See Jefferson's own Summary View.

refused enforcement to a rag-money law on account of
its alleged repugnancy, that is, self-contradictory
character.

Coming, then, to the early State constitutions, we
find coöperating with the influence of Blackstone, to
exclude judicial review from them, two other circumstances: first, uncertainty whether these constitutions
possessed the force of law and, secondly, the actual
organization of legislative power in them. That the
fundamental principles of right and reason invoked
by Coke were known to the judges and enforceable
by them, at least as principles of interpretation in applying statute law, there could of course be no doubt.
For even Blackstone conceded that. But the early
State constitutions were of a different stamp,—they
were acts of revolution, social compacts, sprung from
the pages of Locke rather than of Coke. Undoubtedly
they illustrated and realized the doctrine that all just
government rests upon the consent of the governed.
Yet it was a corollary from this doctrine, that a government established upon this foundation had the right
to *govern,* and that this was recoverable by the people
only by another act of revolution. The power of
enacting laws, however, was a function of *government.*
How, then, could constitutions, bills of rights, frames
of government, the work of the people themselves, be
regarded as laws in the strict sense of the term?
Their moral supremacy none doubted, nor yet that a
breach of them by government destroyed its right to
be, but until the *people* should be regarded as having
an *enacting power,* exercisable directly and without

the intervention of their legislative representatives, the *supremacy* of constitutions was a real barrier to their *legality*.[49]

But the second difficulty was even more formidable. A majority of the early State constitutions contained statements, sometimes in very round terms, of Montesquieu's doctrine of the separation of powers; and as against executive power, a supposed monarchical tendency in which was feared, this principle was given detailed application.[50]   Not so, however, as against legislative power.[51]   In the first place, all through colonial times, the legislature had stood for the local interest as against the imperial interest, which had in turn been represented by the governors and the judges. In the second place, the legislative department was supposed to stand nearest to the people.   Finally, *legislative* power was *undefined* power.   As applied against the legislative department, accordingly, all that the principle of the separation of powers originally

[49] On a constitution as an act of revolution, see the remarks of the judges in *Kamper* v. *Hawkins,* Va. Cases 20, ffg.; also, Marshall in *Marbury* v. *Madison;* also, Tucker's Blackstone, I, App. p. 91.   On the lodgment of the function of governing exclusively with the government, see Luther Martin's remarks in his "Genuine Information" (quoted at close of following essay); also, Dr. Benjamin Rush's remarks in his "Address to the People of the United States" (1787) in Niles' Principles and Acts of the Revolution, 234-36.   The idea, indeed, is fundamental to the concept of representative government.

[50] See data in Federalist Nos. 47 and 48.

[51] The position of the legislature in the early State constitutions is described at length by Morey, in Annals of the Am. Acad. of Soc. and Polit. Sc., IX, 398 ffg.; also by Davis, "American Constitutions" in Johns Hopkins University Studies, 3rd Series.

meant was that those who held seats in the legislature should not at the same time hold office in either of the other departments.[52]   But the legislature itself, like the British Parliament and like the colonial legislatures before it, exercised *all kinds of power,* and particularly did it exercise the power of interpreting the standing law and interfering with the course of justice as administered in the ordinary courts;[53] and the only test of its acts deemed available was that they should be passed in the usual form.[54]   In short, as both Madi-

[52] The doctrine of the separation of powers receives recognition in the body of the first Virginia constitution in the following words: "That the legislative, executive, and judiciary departments ˙ shall be distinct; so that neither exercise the powers properly belonging to the other; nor shall any person exercise the powers of more than one of them at the same time," etc.   See also the first New Jersey Constitution, Art. XX; the original North Carolina Constitution, Arts. XXVIII-XXX; the first Pennsylvania Constitution, Sec. 23; the first South Carolina Constitution, Art. X: Thorpe, Am. Charters, Constitutions, etc.

[53] See note at close of this article on Mingling of Legislative and Judicial Powers.

[54] Consider, for example, Jefferson's words in his "Virginia Notes" (cited above):   It is needless for the executive or the judiciary to attempt to oppose the legislature, he says, for then "they put their proceedings into the form of acts of assembly, which will render them obligatory on the other branches." Consider also C. J. Pendleton's words in *Com.* v. *Caton,* 4 Call. 5, 17 (Va., 1782): "How far this court, in whom the judiciary powers may in some sort be said to be concentrated, shall have power to declare the nullity of a law *passed in its forms* by the legislative power without exercising the power of that branch, contrary to the plain terms of the constitution, is indeed a deep, important, and I will add, a tremendous question the decision of which might involve consequences to which gentlemen may not have extended their ideas."

son and Jefferson put the matter later, legislative power was the *vortex* into which all other powers tended to be drawn. Obviously so long as this remained the case, there could be nothing like judicial review.

The period 1780-1787, however, was a period of "constitutional reaction," which mounting gradually till the outbreak of Shays' Rebellion in Massachusetts in the latter part of 1786, then leaped suddenly to its climax in the Philadelphia Convention. The reaction embraced two phases, that of nationalism against State sovereignty, that of private rights against uncontrolled legislative power; but the point of attack in both instances was the State legislature.[55] Yet it should not be imagined for a moment that those who discerned the central fault of "the American political system" gave themselves over merely to idle lamentation. Fortunately no one contended at that date that the existing American constitutions, wrought out as they had

[55]See criticisms passed in the Convention on the notion that the States were sovereign under the Articles of Confederation, in Farrand I, 313-33, 437-79. See also the present writer's National Supremacy, ch. III (Holt & Co., 1913). For the revolt against legislative oppression of private (property) rights, see the elaborate criticism of the recent product of the State legislatures by Madison in 1786, Writings (Hunt Ed.), II, 338 ffg. Also, see his statement on the floor of the Convention, June 6, and afterwards repeated by him elsewhere, that "the necessity of providing more effectually for the security of private rights and the steady dispensation of justice" was one of the objects of the Convention. "Interferences with these," he declared, "were evils which had, more perhaps than anything else, produced this Convention. Was it to be supposed that republican liberty could long exist under the abuses of it practised in some of the States?" See also Federalist Nos. 10 and 44.

been under the stress and urgency of a state of war-
fare, were impossible of improvement.[56] Fortunately,
too, American political inventiveness had by no means
exhausted itself in its first efforts at constitution-
building. Upon this latent talent the problems of the
times acted as incentive and stimulant, eliciting from
it suggestion after suggestion which it needed but the
ripe occasion to erect into institutions composing a
harmonious whole. Some of these suggestions it is
pertinent to enumerate: (1) from Massachusetts and
New Hampshire came the idea of an ordered and
regular procedure for making constitutions, with the
result inevitably of furthering the idea of an enacting
power in the people at large and that of the legal
character of the constitution;[57] (2) from New Jersey,
Connecticut, Virginia, Rhode Island and perhaps New
Hampshire came the idea of judicial review, partly on
the basis of the doctrine of the right of revolution and
partly on the basis of the doctrine of certain principles
fundamental to the Common Law that had found recognition in the State constitutions;[58] (3) from North

[56] See Jefferson's apologia in his Virginia Notes, above cited;
also Rush's "Address" in Principles and Acts, 234-36.

[57] On the making of the revolutionary State constitutions, see
Davis in Johns Hopkins University Studies, 3rd Series, pp. 516
ffg. The legal character of the Massachusetts constitution of
1780 was recognized and enforced by the supreme court of the
State in a series of decisions, in 1780-81, pronouncing slavery
unconstitutional. See G. H. Moore, History of Slavery in
Massachusetts, pp. 200-23. A futile attempt was made to have
the legislature order rehearings in some of these cases. The
petitioners state the grounds of the decisions, ib. 217-8.

[58] See note at close of this article on Alleged Precedents for
Judicial Review antedating the Convention of 1787.

Carolina, just as the Philadelphia Convention was assembling, came the idea of judicial review based squarely on the written constitution and the principle of the separation of powers;[59] (4) from various sources came the idea that legislative power, instead of being governmental power in general, is a *peculiar kind of power;*[60] (5) from various sources came the idea that judicial power, exercised as it habitually was under the guiding influence of Common Law prin-

[59] *Bayard* v. *Singleton,* 1 Martin 42. See note 24, above. Mr. W. S. Carpenter finds from the contemporary newspapers that this case was decided in May, several days before the Philadelphia Convention had actually come together. The attorneys in the case who argued the unconstitutionality of the legislative act were Wm. R. Davie, a N. C. delegate to the Phila. Convention, and James Iredell, later a member of the first bench of the U. S. Sup. Ct.

[60] See especially Madison's words in Fed. No. 47 and Hamilton's in No. 81. The latter are quoted *infra.* See also the Reports of the Pennsylvania Censors, referred to in the note on the Mingling of Legislative and Judicial Powers at the end of this study. The earliest statement of the respective limits of legislative and judicial powers came from the royal governors, in an effort to check the former. See, for example, the message of Gov. Fletcher to the New York Assembly, Apr. 13, 1695: "Laws are to be interpreted by the judges," *i. e.,* the judges alone: Messages from the Governors (of New York) (Lincoln, Ed.), I, 55. For later gubernatorial messages on the same subject, see *ib.* II, 250 (Apr. 27, 1786), and IV, 532 ffg. (Apr. 10, 1850). For some early judicial statements of the notion, see *Bayard* v. *Singleton;* also *Ogden* v. *Witherspoon* and *Ogden* v. *Blackledge,* discussed below. Some later cases on the point are 5 Cow. (N. Y.) 346; 16 N. Y. 432; 99 N. Y. 463; 159 N. Y. 362. But the classic judicial statements of the established doctrine are in the cases of *Dash* v. *Van Kleeck,* 7 Johns. (N. Y.) 477, 488-93, 498, 508-9 (1811); and *Merrill* v. *Sherburne,* 1 N. H. 199-217 (1817). See also Cooley, Constitutional Limitations (2nd Ed.), 173-5.

ciples, was naturally conservative of private rights;[61]
(6) from various sources came the idea that the judiciary must be put in a position to defend its prerogative against the legislative tendency to absorb all
powers, and this idea was connected with the idea of
judicial review both in the relation of *means* and of
end;[62] (7) from the Congress of the Confederation

---

[61] The reception accorded *Trevett* v. *Weeden* has just been
referred to. At this same time Wm. Plumer was writing
(1786): "The aspect of public affairs in this State is gloomy
. . . Yet even in these degenerate days, our courts of law are
firm": Life of Wm. Plumer, p. 166. It was at this time
that the worship of the judiciary began, which was later to
become so conspicuous a feature of the Federalist régime,
leading indeed to the belief on the part of the judges themselves, that they were meant to be the moral guardians of society. See Henry Jones Ford, Rise and Growth of American
Politics, 112-13. Even Jefferson participated in the general
feeling to a certain extent. Writing Madison in 1789, he said:
"The judiciary, if rendered independent and kept strictly to
their own department, merits great confidence for their learning and integrity": Writings (Ford's Ed.) V, 81. Again in
1793, he wrote: "The courts of justice exercise the sovereignty
of this country in judiciary matters, are supreme in these, and
liable neither to control nor opposition from any other branch
of the government": *ib.* VI, 421. Yet in 1805 he approved the
ffg. sentiment, expressed in complaint of Congress' lack of
power to remove judges: "From this defect in the Constitution arise these evil consequences, that many wrongs are daily
done by the courts, to humble, obscure, or poor suitors. . . .
It is a prodigious monster in a free government to see a class
of men set apart, not simply to administer the laws, but who
exercise a legislative and even an executive power, directly in
defiance and contempt-of the Constitution": Phila. Aurora,
Jan. 28, 1805.

[62] See the criticism by the Pennsylvania Council of Censors
(Nov., 1783) against the existing State Constitution: "Because
if the assembly should pass an unconstitutional law and the

came the idea that the Articles of Confederation and treaties made under them were rightfully to be regarded as part and parcel of the law of every State, paramount, moreover, to conflicting acts of the State legislatures and enforceable by the State courts.[63] Probably no one public man of the time shared all these ideas when the Philadelphia Convention met. But the able membership of that famous body was in a position to compare views drawn from every section of the country. Slowly, by process of discussion and conversation, these men, most of them trained in the legal way of thinking, discovered the intrinsic harmony of the ideas just passed in review; discovered, in other words, that the acceptance of one of them more or less constrained the acceptance of the others also, that each implied a system embracing all.

The Virginia Plan, introduced into the Convention at its outset, provided for the three departments of government. None the less, the same plan gave evidence that its authors had but imperfect recognition of the implications of the doctrine of the separation of powers, for it associated members of the judiciary in a council with the executive to revise measures of the national legislature and it left to the

judges have the virtue to disobey it, the same could instantly remove them": *loc cit.*, p. 70. See also, Hamilton in Federalist Nos. 78 and 80; also *infra* on the debate of 1802. Madison's anxiety for judicial independence of legislative influence was extreme: Farrand II, 44-5.

[63] Secret Journals of Congress (1821), IV, 185-287; Journals of Congress (1801), XII, under dates of Mar. 21 and Apr. 13, 1787. See also, *Bayard* v. *Singleton* (supra) and Writings of Jefferson (Mem. Ed.), VI, 98.

national legislature the task of keeping State legislation subordinate to national powers. The first important step in the clarification of the Convention's
ideas with reference to the doctrine of judicial review
is marked, therefore, by its rejection of the Council
of Revision idea on the basis of the principle stated
perhaps most precisely by Strong of Massachusetts,
"That the power of *making* ought to be kept distinct
from that of *expounding* the laws." "No maxim,"
Strong added, "was better established," and the utter-
ances of other members bear out his words.[64] For, in
one form or another, the notion of legislative power as
inherently limited power, distinct from and exclusive
of the power of interpreting the standing law, was
reiterated again and again and was never contradicted. When, therefore, the Convention adopted
Article III of the Constitution vesting "the judicial
power of the United States in one Supreme Court
and such inferior courts as Congress shall from time
to time establish," it must be regarded as having expressed the intention of excluding Congress from the
business of law-interpreting altogether.

But a not less important step toward the final result
was taken when the idea of a congressional veto of
State laws was dropped and for it was substituted
the Small State proposition of giving the Constitution
the character of supreme law within the individual
States enforceable by the several State judiciaries.[65]

[64] Farrand II, 73-80.

[65] Note particularly the significance of Sherman's words with
reference to congressional veto: "Such a power involves a
wrong principle, to wit, that a law of a State contrary to the

Thus it was settled that as against State legislation at any rate the Constitution should be *legally* supreme. Why not then as against national legislation as well? When it was decided that the Constitution should be referred for ratification to conventions within the States, the question was probably determined for the majority of the members. Said Madison: "A law violating a constitution established by the people themselves would be considered by the judges as null and void."[66] Later the Convention proceeded to insert in the Constitution prohibitions upon congressional power in the same terms as some of those already imposed upon State legislative power.[67] The conclusion is unescapable that when Article VI, par. 2, designates the Constitution as *law* of the land in the same terms as it does acts of Congress made in pursuance of it, it does so by virtue of no inadvertence or inattention on the part of its framers. Moreover, as noted before, the same paragraph recognizes State constitutions as known to and enforceable by State courts.

But then was it upon the premises thus provided that the Convention did actually base its belief in judicial review of acts of Congress? The answer to this question is indicated in part by the fact that the func-

Articles of Union would, if not negatived, be valid and operative." Yet as late as Aug. 23, John Langdon of New Hampshire said: "He considered it [the question of a Congressional veto] resolvable into the question whether the extent of the National Constitution was to be judged of by the State governments": Farrand II, 391. The "arising" clause was adopted Aug. 27.

[66] Farrand, II, 93.

[67] Cf. sections 9 and 10 of Art. I.

tion of judicial review is almost invariably related by the members of the Convention to the power of the judges as "expositors of the law." But a better rounded and a more satisfactory answer is furnished by Hamilton's argument in Federalist 78: *"The interpretation of the laws is the proper and peculiar province of the courts. A constitution is in fact, and must be regarded by the judges, as a fundamental law. It therefore belongs to them to ascertain its meaning as well as the meaning of any particular act proceeding from the legislative body, and, in case of irreconcilable difference between the two, to prefer the will of the people declared in the constitution to that of the legislature as expressed in statute."* It cannot be reasonably doubted that Hamilton was here, as at other points, endeavoring to reproduce the matured conclusions of the Convention itself.[68] And not less certain is it that he was thus notifying those to whom the Constitution had been referred for ratification of the grounds upon which its framers and supporters based the case for judicial review.

[68] Note also the words of James Wilson in his "Lectures" (1792), where he presents judicial review as "the necessary result of the distribution of power made by the Constitution between the legislative and the judicial departments": Works (Andrews' Ed.), I, 416-7. Note, too, the words with which Hamilton introduces his discussion of the grounds of judicial review: "As this *doctrine* is of great importance in *all* the Am. constitutions, a brief discussion of the *grounds* on which it rests cannot be unacceptable." There is, in other words, no *peculiar* foundation for the power in the U. S. Constitution.

V

Our demonstration, however, of the views of the framers with reference to the basis of judicial review may also be profitably extended to the period between the adoption of the Constitution and the decision in *Marbury* v. *Madison*. For this was the period when the new system was set going, not only in the still un-dimmed light of the views of its authors, but for the most part under their personal supervision. But the interest of the period also arises in part from the real paradox which judicial review has always presented in our system from the outset, the paradox namely of try-ing to keep a government based on public opinion within the metes and bounds of a formally unchange-able law. The dilemma thus created did not at first press, but with the rise of political opposition it became grave enough, and when this opposition finally tri-umphed, not only judicial review but even judicial independence was for the moment in peril.

But, indeed, the difficulty at the time of the adop-tion of the Constitution was hardly a new one, for some such objection had been earlier forthcoming to judicial review within the States themselves, where however, the judges were generally much less secure of independence than under the United States Constitu-tion,[68a] and where, as we have seen, the legislature still freely directed the course of judicial proceedings. Furthermore, as I have already indicated, judicial re-view as at first proposed for the States had rested upon a logic which put it in the light of a highly extra-

[68a] See the data given in Annals of Congress, I, col. 844.

ordinary, quasi-revolutionary remedy, and gave it sway within the very limited area marking the intersection, so to speak, of the written constitution with fundamental principles of the Common Law.

It is hardly surprising, then, to find Hamilton turning from his work of planting judicial review squarely within the Constitution and of rendering its field of operation co-extensive with the four corners of that instrument, to consider certain objections, which he recites as follows:

"The authority of the proposed Supreme Court of the United States, which is to be a separate and independent body, will be superior to that of the legislature. The power of construing the laws according to the spirit of the Constitution will enable that court to mould them into whatever shape it may think proper; especially as its decisions will not be in any manner subject to the revision or correction of the legislative body. This is as unprecedented as it is dangerous. . . . The Parliament of Great Britain and the legislatures of the several States can at any time rectify by law the exceptionable decisions of their respective courts. But the errors and usurpations of the Supreme Court of the United States will be uncontrollable and remediless."

Hamilton met these objections by flatly denying that the principle of the separation of powers permitted even a State legislature to reverse a judicial decree. Said he: "Neither the theory of the British nor the State constitutions authorizes the revisal of a judicial sentence by a legislative act."[69]

Madison, on the other hand, responded—characteristically—to the views of the alarmists more pro-

---

[69] Federalist No. 81. Hamilton also pointed to impeachment as an available remedy for an abuse of power by the judges.

nouncedly. On the floor of the Convention, as we have just seen, he had espoused the doctrine of judicial review in unmistakable terms. Again in the Federalist he had described the Supreme Court as the tribunal which was "ultimately to decide" the questions that would necessarily arise between the State and national jurisdictions.[70] And in the Virginia convention his point of view had still been the same: the National Government was to be the final judge of its own powers through the Supreme Court.[71] Yet within six months he was writing a correspondent in Kentucky that neither the federal nor State constitutions made any provision "for the case of a disagreement in expounding them" and that the attempt of the courts to stamp a law "with its final character" "by refusing or not refusing to execute it" made "the judicial department paramount in fact to the legislative, which was never intended and can never be proper."[72]

Still Madison was reluctant to abandon judicial review outright. What he really desired was a principle which, while saving to judicial interpretations of the Constitution their finality in certain instances, in

[70] No. 39.

[71] Elliot, III, 484-5.

[72] Note 35, *supra*. Madison, like many other Virginians of prominence, was angered at this time by the pedantic attitude taken by the State court of appeals toward an act of the legislature imposing new duties on them without increasing their salaries. See the Case of the Judges, 4 Call. 139, ffg. (1788). The case gave rise to a vigorous debate in the Virginia assembly. See Monroe to Madison, Nov. 22, 1788: "Letters to Madison," MSS., Library of Congress.

others clad those of Congress with a like finality. He soon had an opportunity to attempt the formulation of such a principle. The bill introduced into the first Congress creating the Department of Foreign Affairs contained the clause, with reference to the Secretary of State, "to be removable from office by the President of the United States." The clause was at once attacked by Smith of South Carolina in the following words: "What authority has this house to explain the law? . . . Sir, it is the duty of the legislature to make laws; your judges are to expound them." • Madison sprang to the defense of the clause. He admitted that it represented an attempt by Congress to construe the Constitution *finally* at the point involved, but he asserted that it was within Congress' power to do this very thing in a case where the Constitution was silent and the question raised concerned an apportionment of power among departments. In other words, an assumed incompleteness at points was to give Congress its opportunity. But, rejoined Gerry of Massachusetts,

"I would ask, gentlemen, if the Constitution has given us the the power to make declaratory acts, where is the necessity of inserting the Fifth Article for the purpose of obtaining amendments? The word amendment implies a defect, a declaratory act conceives one. Where then is the difference between an amendment and a declaratory act?"

The protest against an "attempt to construe the Constitution" was also voiced by Sherman of Connecticut, Page and White of Virginia, and Benson of New York, with the result that eventually Madison himself joined in support of a motion striking out the exceptionable clause and substituting for it phraseology merely inferring that the President would exercise the power of removal and making provision for the event.[73] A little later the House passed the Judiciary Act almost without comment upon the 25th section of it, which recognizes the judicial prerogative in relation to the written constitution in the most explicit fashion.[74]

[73] For this debate, see Annals of Congress, I, col. 473 ffg.

[74] The following are the names of those who attended the Philadelphia Convention and later supported the Act of 1789: Ellsworth, Paterson, Strong, Bassett, and Few--all of whom were on the Senate Committee that drafted the act; Robert Morris and Read, also Senators; and Madison, Baldwin, and Sherman in the House.   Professor Beard in his Supreme Court, etc., assumes that all these men must have favored judicial review in 1787.   The argument must be taken with considerable allowance, for judicial review was a rapidly spreading idea during this period.   On the floor of the Convention itself there were several converts.   Read, for example, in this connection the exact statements of Gerry, Wilson, and Dickinson, as reported by Madison.   Compare Dickinson in his "Letters of Fabius."   Compare Morris' words in 1785: Sparks, Life of Gouverneur Morris, III, 438.   Mr. Horace Davis in the November, 1913, Am. Polit. Sc. Rev. seeks to prove, on the other hand, that those who supported the Act of 1789 thereby showed that they did not believe in the power of the Supreme Court to pass upon the validity of acts of Congress, except as the question was raised in cases coming up from the State courts.   If Mr. Davis had turned to the debate, just reviewed, on the establishment of the Department of Foreign Affairs, he would have found at least half a dozen men championing the notion of judicial review who later voted for the Act of 1789.   Also, I should like to ask where the State courts get their power to pass on the validity of acts of Congress save as it is intrinsic to judicial power under a constitution regarded as law.   The argument would, however, have considerable force if the Supreme Court got its power from the clause "cases arising under

From this time on for nearly a decade, the juristic view of the Constitution passed substantially without challenge. It is true that when in the first Hayburn case the judges of the Middle Circuit refused to enforce the Pension Act of 1792 on the ground of its unconstitutionality, some "high-fliers in and out of Congress" raised the cry of impeachment; but they were speedily silenced. Upon the objections of the judges to the act being filed with the President, the latter forwarded them to Congress, which proceeded promptly to bring the act into conformity with the judicial view of constitutional requirements.[75]   Four

this Constitution," considered in the light of Hamilton's interpretation of it in Fed. 80. For some further references in the first Congress to judicial review, see Annals, I, cols. 457, 763, 767-8; II, cols. 1978 and 1988.

[75] The materials for this account of the "Pension Case" are drawn from 2 Dall. 409; Am. St. Papers, Misc. I, 49-52; Annals of Cong., III, cols. 556-7; Annals of Cong., XI (7th Cong., 1st sess'n), cols. 921-5; *U. S.* v. *Ferreira,* 13 How. 40 (note). The statement with reference to the threat of impeachment is based on the following extract from Bache's General Advertiser (Camden, N. J. for Apr. 20, 1792): "Never was the word 'impeachment' so hackneyed as it has been since the spirited sentence passed by our judges on an unconstitutional law. The high-fliers, in and out of Congress, and the very humblest of their humble retainers, talk of nothing but impeachment! impeachment! impeachment! as if forsooth Congress were wrapped up in the cloak of infallibility, which has been torn from the shoulders of the Pope; and that it was damnable heresy and sacrilege to doubt the constitutional orthodoxy of any decision of theirs, once written on calf skin! But if a Secretary of War can suspend or reverse the decision of the Circuit Judges, why may not a drill sergeant or a black drummer reverse the decisions of a jury? Why not abolish at once all our Courts, except the court martial? and burn all our laws, except the articles of war . . . ?" "But when those

years later occurred the case of *United States* v. *Hylton*,[76] which is instructive of the established doctrine in a number of ways. The only question argued before the court was that of the constitutionality of the act of Congress involved. In the argument for the United States, the Attorney General was assisted by Alexander Hamilton, for whose services Congress appropriated a special fund. Neither side challenged the power of the court in the premises.[77] The court's decision upholding the act was based purely upon the merits of the case. Madison was plainly disappointed at the act's not being disallowed.[78]

And meantime, judicial review was also advancing within the States, and what is an even more significant development, was being transferred from the earlier basis of fundamental principles to the written consti-

---

impeachment mongers are asked how any law is to be declared unconstitutional, they tell us that nothing less than a general convention is adequate to pass sentence on it; as if a general convention could be assembled with as much ease as a party of stock jobbers." And to like effect is a paragraph in Freneau's National Gazette for Apr. 16, 1792. I am indebted for these references to my friend, Mr. W. S. Carpenter, who is preparing a volume on Judicial Tenure in the United States.

[76] 3 Dall. 171 (1796).

[77] Annals, XI, cols. 925-6.

[78] It was also during this period that, in 1793, the Supreme Court refused Washington's request to advise him with reference to the operation of the treaties of 1778 with France, basing its refusal upon the strictly judicial character of their office: Baldwin, American Judiciary, 33. In the debate on the Department of Foreign Affairs in 1789, Gerry had expressed the idea that the President could require opinions of the judges on constitutional questions and that these would be binding on Congress: *loc. cit.* col. 524.

tution. Two illustrative cases are *Bowman* v. *Middleton*,[79] and *Kamper* v. *Hawkins*.[80] In the former, decided in 1792, the South Carolina supreme court pronounced an early colonial statute to have been void *ab initio* as contrary to "common right" and "Magna Carta." In the latter, four years later, the Virginia court of appeals pronounced an act of the State legislature void as in conflict with the letter and spirit of the Virginia constitution, which was described as an ordinance of the people themselves and therefore superior to an ordinary statute, but as nonetheless a source of rules determinative of the rights of individuals.[81]

One thing that retarded the growth of judicial review in the States was the continuing influence of Blackstone, with his notion of parliamentary sovereignty,[82] but a not less potent factor was the

[79] 1 Bay (S. C.) 252. Earlier than this, in the case of *Ham* v. *McClaws, loc. cit.,* 93 (1789), the S. C. court, following Coke's dictum, gave a statute a very restricted meaning to bring it into conformity with "rules of common right and justice." "Statutes made against natural equity," said the court, "are void, and so also are statutes made against Magna Carta."

[80] Va. Cases, 20.

[81] Note J. Nelson's words, p. 131 of the volume: For the legislature to decide whether its own act is void or not would be unconstitutional, "since to decide whether the plaintiff or defendant under the existing law have a right is a judicial act."

[82] For an illustration of the Blackstonian influence, see Zephaniah Swift, The System of Laws of Connecticut (1795), pp. 16-7, 34-5, 52-3. Also, in the same connection, see arguments of attorneys in 4 Halstead (N. J.) 427 and 1 Binney (Pa.) 416. For a decidedly disingenuous and somewhat amusing attempt to explain Blackstone's words away, see Works of James Wilson (Andrews' Ed.), II, 415. Note also, Marshall's

retention of the doctrine that legislative power extended to the interpretation of the standing law. Thus as late as 1798 we find Justice Chase of the United States Supreme Court declaring that only in the Massachusetts constitution were the *powers* of government *distributed;* and two years later the same judge announced his opinion that the mere statement of the general principle of the separation of powers in a State constitution did not serve to restrict the legislative powers, that such general principles were "not to be regarded as rules to fetter and control, but as matter merely declaratory and directory."[83]   But in *Ogden* v. *Witherspoon,*[84] which was a North Carolina case falling within federal jurisdiction because of the diverse citizenship of the parties to it, and in which therefore the federal court stood in the same relation to the State constitution that the State court would have, Chief Justice Marshall on circuit reversed this position; and in *Ogden* v. *Blackledge* the Supreme Court itself sustained his course.   In the latter case the question at issue was whether a North Carolina

words, as attorney in *Ware* v. *Hylton,* 3 Dall. 199, 211: "The judicial authority have no right to question the validity of a law unless such a jurisdiction is given expressly by the constitution."

[83] The cases referred to are *Calder* v. *Bull,* 3 Dall. 386, and *Cooper* v. *Telfair,* 4 Dall. 13.   Justice Chase indicates by his remarks in these cases, significantly, reluctance to admit judicial review save on the basis of natural rights and the social compact.   His remarks in the latter case, however, contain interesting testimony as to the unanimity of opinion on the subject among bench and bar, both in 1800 and at the time of the adoption of the Constitution.

[84] 3 N. C. 404 (1802).

statute of limitations, passed in 1715, had been repealed in 1789, the State legislature having declared
in 1799 that it had not been.   Said attorney for
plaintiff: "To declare what the law is or has been
is a judicial power, to declare what it shall be is
legislative.   One of the fundamental principles of all
our governments is that the legislative power shall be
separated from the judicial."[85]   The court stopped
counsel and decided that, "under all the circumstances
stated, the act in question had been repealed in 1789."

The service thus rendered the cause of judicial review
under the State constitutions by the federal courts
acting in their vicarious capacity cannot be overesti-
mated.   By 1820, the spread of the juristic interpretation of the principle of the separation of powers
had effected the establishment of judicial review on
the basis of the written constitution in every State in
the Union save only Rhode Island, which exception
moreover only proves the rule, since it is explained by
the fact that till 1842 Rhode Island continued its
colonial charter as a constitution and that by this instrument legislative power remained undefined.   Nonetheless, even today, State judges in exercising this
power sometimes place their right to it upon a somewhat precarious basis.[86]

VI

But lastly we turn to consider the challenge made
to the finality of the Supreme Court's interpretation

[85] 2 Cr. 272, 276 (1805).

[86] See the note at the close of this study on the Establishment
of Judicial Review in the States.

of the Constitution in relation to acts of Congress by
Jefferson and his more radical followers in the years
1798-1802. The matter most immediately demanding
explanation is evident. It is the entire failure of
this challenge even while its authors were borne into
higher office by an overwhelming political triumph.

The debate and vote on the Judiciary Act of 1789
prove that originally the advocates of State rights—
for they existed from the beginning—were nothing
loath to accept the Supreme Court's view of the Constitution as final, both in relation to national and to
State power. When, however, the federal judges
showed themselves disposed to uphold and enforce
the Alien and Sedition Laws of 1798, and some of
them indeed to entertain prosecutions for sedition
under a supposed Common Law of the United States,[86a]
the State-rights champions began to appreciate for
the first time the added sanction given to national
authority by judicial decision. The Virginia and
Kentucky Resolutions of 1798 and 1799 were framed
primarily with the design of breaking through this
subtle control, on the warrant of the propositions,
first that the Constitution was a compact of sovereign
States and, second, that the organ of sovereignty within
a State was its legislature, from which propositions
the conclusion was drawn that the final word in construing the national Constitution lay with the indi-

[86a] On the question of whether the federal courts enjoy a
Common Law jurisdiction independently of statute, see *U. S.* v.
Worrall, 2 Dall. 384; *U. S.* v. *Hudson et al.,* 7 Cr. 32; *U. S.*
v. *Coolidge,* 1 Gall. 488.

vidual State legislatures.[87]   But the outcome of
the propaganda thus undertaken was not merely a
further vindication of the prerogative of the Supreme
Court of the United States, but of *all* courts.   Thus
having been forwarded to the other legislatures, the
resolutions elicited from the seven Northern of them
unequivocal declarations of the right of the "Supreme
Court of the United States ultimately" to decide "on
the constitutionality of any act" of Congress.[88]   In his
famous Report of 1799 to the Virginia legislature,
Madison endeavored at first to meet these responses
by reiterating the doctrine of the original resolutions,
but even in so doing he admitted the finality of judicial constructions of the Constitution as against the
other branches of the National Government, and in
the end he abandoned his case completely.[89]   The
Resolutions, he contended, taking a defensive tone,
were entirely proper, since they were designed merely
"to excite reflection," whereas, he added, decisions of
the judiciary, *"are carried into immediate effect by
force."*   It would be hard to imagine a more complete
retreat.   The probability is that he and those for
whom he spoke had begun to realize that to make the
State legislature the final interpreter of the National

[87] MacDonald, Select Documents, 148-60; Elliot, IV., 528-32,
540-45. It should be noted that Jefferson did not deny judicial
review outright in 1798.   Writing Rowan, Sept. 26, 1798, he
said: "The laws of the land, administered by upright judges
would protect you from any exercise of power unauthorized
by the Constitution of the U. S.": Writings (Ford, Ed.),
VII, 281.
[88] H. V. Ames, State Documents on Federal Relations, 16-26.
[89] Writings (Hunt's Ed.), VI, 341-406.

Constitution was also to make it the final interpreter ⟵
of the State constitution, which in turn meant either
the setting up of a legally uncontrolled power within
the State itself or—what *practically* would have been
the same thing—return to the idea, now rapidly becoming obsolete, of a legislative function of *jus dicere*.

Two years later, nevertheless, the question of the
finality of the judicial view of the Constitution was
again to the front, though on a somewhat altered footing. By the election of 1800 the Republicans had
captured the Presidency and both Houses of Congress,
but the judiciary still withstood them. Now, at the
very moment of retiring from power the Federalists
proceeded by the Act of February, 1801, substantially
to double the number of inferior federal courts, while
President Adams at once set to work, with the co-
operation of the Senate, to fill the newly created offices
with Federalists. The federal judiciary, exclaimed
Randolph wrathfully, has become "a hospital of de-
cayed politicians!" Jefferson's concern went deeper.
Writing Dickinson he said: "They have retired into
the judiciary, from which stronghold they will batter
down all the works of Republicanism."

Naturally the first step attempted was the repeal
of the Act of 1801, but from the point of view of a
possible larger program of definitely subordinating
the judiciary to the political branches of the government, the repeal voted was indeed a Pyrrhic victory.[90]

[90] Jefferson and Giles were originally of the opinion that the
act was irrepealable. They were converted to their later view
by the dialectic of John Taylor of Caroline. These statements
are based on documents from the Breckenridge MSS. which

In the debate on the question the Federalists speedily developed the argument that, inasmuch as the Constitution designed the judiciary to act as a check upon Congress, the latter was under constitutional obligation not to weaken the independence of the former in any way. To meet this argument Breckenridge of Kentucky, the Republican leader in the Senate—and one of the authors of the Kentucky Resolutions— brought forward the theory of the equal right of the three departments, when acting within their respective fields, to construe the Constitution for themselves, and from it deduce the exclusive right of the legislature "to interpret the Constitution in what regards the law-making power" and the obligation of the judges "to execute what laws they make." In other words, as we noted earlier, the notion of a departmental right of constitutional construction takes its rise not from the effort to establish judicial review but from an attempt to overthrow it. But the feeble disguise which this doctrine affords legislative sovereignty made it little attractive even to Republicans, who for the most part either plainly indicated their adherence to the juristic view of the Constitution, or following a hint by Giles of Virginia, kept silent on the subject. The Federalists on the other hand were unanimous on the main question, though of divergent opinions as to the grounds on which judicial review was to be legally based, some grounding it on the "arising" and "pursuant" clauses, some on the precedents of the Pension and Carriage

are given in Mr. W. S. Carpenter's thesis on Judicial Tenure in the United States.

cases, some on the nature of the Constitution and of
the judicial office, some on "the contemporary use of
terms" and "the undisputed practice under the Constitution" "of all constitutional authorities." And undoubtedly, by this date, all these grounds were fairly
available save the first. For the rest, said the Federalist orators, judicial review was expedient, since the
judiciary had control of neither the purse nor the
sword; it was the substitute offered by political wis-
dom for the destructive right of revolution; "to have
established this principle of constitutional security,"
"a novelty in the history of nations," was "the peculiar
glory of the American people;" the contrary doctrine
was "monstrous and unheard of."[91]

[91] Annals of Cong., XI, cols. 26-184 (Senate), cols. 510-985
(House). Breckenridge of Kentucky did not at first attack
judicial review, *loc. cit.* 92-9; but was finally prodded to it, *ib.*
178-80. In the Senate two advocates of repeal attacked judicial
review (Breckenridge and Stone of North Carolina), while two
(Jackson of Georgia and Wright of Maryland) accepted it.
In the House, three advocates of repeal attacked judicial review (Randolph of Virginia, Williams of North Carolina, and
Thompson of Virginia); two endeavored to discover a compromise position, along the line of the doctrine of departmental
equality (Davis of Kentucky and Bacon of Massachusetts);
but five, impliedly at least, accepted judicial review without
making such qualifications (Smith of Vermont, Nicholson of
Maryland, Gregg of Pennsylvania, Holland of North Carolina,
and Varnum of Massachusetts). Their remarks can be easily
located through the Index. Those of Randolph and Bacon are
most instructive. In the Senate, seven opponents of repeal
championed judicial review (see, especially, the speeches of
Morris of New York, and Chipman of Vermont). In the
House, fifteen of the same party performed this service. The
remarks quoted in the text are from the speeches of Stanly and
Henderson of North Carolina, Rutledge of South Carolina, and

A few months later occurred the decision in *Marbury* v. *Madison,* which against this background assumes its true color. Yet Marshall's performance is by no means to be regarded as a work of supererogation. In the first place, vested as it was with the apparent authority of a judicial decision, it brought to an end a discussion which, for all that it had been highly favorable to judicial review, might in the end have proved unsettling. Again, it threw the emphasis once more upon the great essential considerations of the character of the Constitution, as "fundamental and paramount law" and "the province and duty of the judicial department to say what the law is." Finally, in the very process of vindicating judicial review, it admitted to a degree the principle that had thus far been contended for only by opponents of judicial review. Thus, discussing the amenability of the President and his agents to mandamus, the Chief Justice says: "By the Constitution of the United States the President is vested with certain important political powers in the exercise of which he is to use his own discretion and is accountable only to his country in

Dana of Connecticut: Cols. 529-30, 542-3, 547-6, 754-5, 920, 932. Other notable speeches were those of Goddard and Griswold of Connecticut, and Hemphill of Pennsylvania. Giles' case is interesting. In the debate on the first Bank, 1791, he had answered an argument in behalf of the proposition, that was drawn from the fact that the Congress of the Confederacy had chartered "the Bank of North America" thus: "The act itself was never confirmed by a judicial decision." In other words, adjudication is made the final test of constitutionality. But in 1804, we find him holding that Congress might impeach a judge for declaring one of its acts unconstitutional: J. Q. Adams, Memoirs, I, 321 ffg.

his political character and to his own conscience."[92]
Later of course, this doctrine, which we may call the
doctrine of *departmental discretion,* was supplemented
by the doctrine that the powers of Congress must be
liberally construed,[93] and later still by the doctrine of
the immunity of the President from judicial process.[94]
All these doctrines may be readily harmonized with
the theory of judicial review.[95]   At the same time,
they are not constrained by that theory, but are plainly
concessions to the necessity of making the Constitution flexible and adaptable while still keeping it legal.
They prove therefore that "the spirit of accommodation" with which Professor McLaughlin credits the
political departments has at least been met by a similar
spirit on the part of the judiciary.

*   *   *   *

Judicial Review originally offered itself on the
basis of the notion of Fundamental Law, but could
not establish itself on that basis because legislative
power was still undefined, approximating indeed to
all governmental power viewed in the light of its
exercise by a particular organ of government.   Later
the emergence of the distinction between law as an
act of revelation, like the Common Law, and law
as an act of authority, like statute law, suggested the

[92] 1 Cr. 165-6.
[93] *McCulloch* v. *Md.,* 4 Wheat. 316 (1819).
[94] *Miss.* v. *Johnson,* 4 Wall. 475 (1867).
[95] The theory, however, of the immunity of the President from
jurisdiction for his personal and private acts, so long as he
remains in office, has no reasonable foundation.   See in this
connection Countryman, The Supreme Court and its Appellate
Jurisdiction, pp. 230 ffg. (Albany, 1913).

requisite differentiation of "legislative" and "judicial" powers; but this distinction was accompanied by the notion of legislative sovereignty, and so judicial review was once again postponed.[96] But in democratic America the attribute of sovereignty was presently absorbed by the People,—first, in its passive sense of the *source* of governing power, and later in its active sense of the *highest* governing power; and the result of the latter development was to impart to the constitution the character, not simply of an act of revolution, but of *law,* in the true sense of the term of a source of rules enforceable by the courts.

Until the Convention of 1787, judicial review as a workable institution was still *in ovo.* One of the main motives however that had brought the Convention together was a general disgust at the recent antics of the State legislatures. To curtail legislative power as it existed in the State constitutions in the interest, first, of an adequate national power and, secondly, in the interest of private rights, was therefore one of the main problems before that body. From some of the States, the tentative hint of judicial review was available, and when the notion of a congressional veto on State laws was rejected, was gladly turned to. But this outcome had in fact been substantially

[96] Note in this general connection that James Otis maintained in his Rights. of the British Colonists Asserted and Proved (1764) that, "The supreme power in a state is *jus dicere* only; *jus dare,* strictly speaking, belongs only to God": McLaughlin, The Courts, etc., p. 70. With Otis' contention, on the other hand, compare Bacon's significant warning in his Essay on Judicature, that the judges ought to be "lions, but lions under the throne" and not to "interfere with points of sovereignty."

guaranteed from the first by the Convention's grow-
ing comprehension of the principle of *the separation
of powers* in relation to *a written constitution regarded as law;* and by the same token, judicial review of acts of Congress was also assured from an
early date a place in the projected system.

From time to time, various other arguments than
the one just reiterated have been urged in support of
judicial review, even by judges, particularly of the
State courts; but they are all invalid as assuming the
very point in dispute. The judges do not exercise a
revolutionary function in pronouncing acts of the
legislature void, but an official function. Their constitutional equality with the other departments se-
cures them in the possession of their rightful powers
but does not enlarge those powers. Their oath of
fidelity to the constitution does not oblige them to exercise other than their constitutional powers in its
defense. Furthermore, the notion of an equal authority in all departments and officers to determine the
meaning of the constitution for themselves was originally brought forward with a view to *checking* judicial
review.

And thus much by way of summary. In the last
analysis, the doctrine of judicial review involves "an
act of Faith," to wit, the belief that the judges *really
know* the standing law and that they *alone* know it.[97]

---

[97] Says Montesquieu: "Judges are no more than the mouth
that pronounces the words of the law." Mr. Pope in his article
in the Harv. Law Rev., cited above, insists upon the belief in
1787 that the judges *knew* the law, while all others had only
opinions about it.

This act of faith was easy for the popular mind under the régime of the Common Law. To-day, however, through the activity of legislatures in the prosecution of Reform, law comes to be looked upon more and more as something *made* rather than as something *discovered,*—as an act of *authority* rather than as an act of *knowledge*. The result is that the possibility of an automatic declaration of the law by the judges comes to be regarded with scepticism; and it comes to be said that the judges in interpreting the law really change it and in interpreting the constitution really change that.

To these views a large measure of truth must be conceded. Meantime, fortunately, the philosophy of Evolution has introduced a distinction of palpable serviceability to our constitutional theory in its present exigency, the distinction between *growth by gradual accretion* and *change by leaps and bounds*. The concept of an automatic declaration of the law is therefore no longer necessary to the doctrine of the separation of powers. The judges change the law, it is true, but they go about the business in a vastly different way than the legislature does. The legislature acts simply upon considerations of expediency. The judges are controlled by precedent, logic, the sensible meaning of words, and their perception of moral consequences.[98]

Also, as it happens, our courts are to-day in a position in construing the constitution to avail them-

[98] See generally Prof. Vinogradoff's illuminating little volume on Common Sense in Law (Home Univ. Library Series, Holt & Co. N. Y., 1914).

selves of the modern flexible view of law as something *inherently* developing, in a way never before
possible to them. All constitutional limitations setting the bounds between the rights of the community
and the rights of the individual have tended of recent
years to be absorbed into the constitutional requirement of "due process of law" and this requirement,
in turn, has come to take on the general meaning of
"reasonable law."[99] So far as constitutional theory
itself is concerned there is small ground for the com-
plaints levelled by reformers at judicial review. When,
however, one turns to the more concrete matter of the
fitness of particular judges for the great responsibility vested in them by the constitution, there is, of
course, often room for discussion.

Notes

I—Judicial Review in the State Ratifying Conventions: The power that the courts would have with
reference to unconstitutional acts of Congress was expounded at length in the Pa. convention by Wilson:
Elliot, Debates, II, 417, 454 (Edition of 1836); also by
Ellsworth in the Conn. convention, *ib*. 198-9. It was
referred to directly by Hamilton in the N. Y. convention,
ib. 336-7. Several references occur to it in the N. C.
convention that failed to ratify; *loc. cit.* IV, 87, 93-4,
152, 165, 167, 192. The report of the debate in the
Mass. Convention on the judiciary appears in only very
abbreviated form on account of the illness of the reporter
at this stage of the proceedings. But Samuel Adams
made a direct allusion to the power of judicial review
affecting acts of Congress; *loc. cit.* II, 142; and other
speakers used language showing their recognition of
some such power in courts; see *ib*. 97-8, 100-6, 110-11,
138, 154, 167, 171-4. In the Va. convention, judicial

---

[99] See the present writer in 7 Mich. Law Rev., 543 ffg.

review was referred to, either as touching acts of Congress or in more general terms, no fewer than twelve times: *loc. cit.* III, 182 and 309 (Henry); 197, 208, and 431 (Randolph); 287 and 498 (Pendleton); 409 (Nicholas); 441 (Mason); 484-5 (Madison);' 503 (Marshall); 514 (Granger). Much of this and further evidence is presented by Mr. Horace Davis in his article in the Am. Pol. Sc. Rev. Mr. Davis himself, however, endeavors to reject the obvious verdict of this evidence. The explanation of his attitude is that he confuses the question of whether judicial review of acts of Congress was believed to be a feature of the new system with the question whether it was expected to prove an effective limitation upon Congress. The absence of a Bill of Rights and the presence of the "general welfare" and "necessary and proper" clauses caused opponents of the Constitution to charge that the judges would never be able to stamp any act of Congress as invalid, that Congress' power was practically unlimited to begin with. See Elliot, I, 545; II, 314-15, 318, 321-2; IV, 175; also, McMaster and Stone, Pennsylvania and the Federal Constitution, 467, 611; also, Ford, Pamphlets, 312; also and especially, Federalist No. 33. Said Whitehill in the Pa. convention: "Laws may be made in *pursuance* of the Constitution, though not *agreeably* to it; the laws may be unconstitutional": McMaster and Stone, *loc. cit.* 780.

II—The Doctrine of Departmental Construction of the Constitution. There is an early hint of this doctrine in Jefferson's Va. Notes, which is criticized by Madison in Fed. No. 49. A much more explicit statement of the doctrine is that of Abraham Baldwin in the U. S. Senate, Jan. 23, 1800: Farrand, III, 383. For Jefferson's view formulated late in life, see his Writings (Mem. Ed.), XV, 212 ffg. Madison as President took the position that he had no discretion in the matter of enforcing, not only decisions of the judiciary, but acts of Congress: Am. St. Papers, Misc., II, 12 (1809). Professor McLaughlin, on the other hand, refers approvingly to old Gideon Welles' attempt "to make General Grant see that he was not under constitutional obligation to obey an act if that act

was unconstitutional. Grant maintained that he was
under obligations to obey a law until the Supreme Court
declared it unconstitutional. Such is the natural position of the layman." But even Welles had no idea of
maintaining that the President would not be bound by a
decision of the Supreme Court: Diary of Gideon
Welles, III, 176-80. Furthermore, on the precise question in issue between Welles and Grant, I must express a
preference for the views of the latter. Obedience to the
mandates of the legislature till they are proved to be
void is one of the risks of office under our system. The
contrary view leads to irresponsibility and disorder.
Lincoln's views expressed in criticism of the Dred Scott
decision reveal some contradictions: see Haines, 265-9.
Lincoln himself virtually admitted that, in disobeying the
mandate of the court in Merryman's case he had violated
the Constitution in one particular, but pleaded the necessity he had been under to do so in order to save it as
a whole. But then, is the President *always* bound to
take the measure of his powers from the Supreme
Court? The answer is, that by the Supreme Court's
own view of the Constitution many of the powers vested
by it in the President are to be exercised at his discretion: *Martin* v. *Mott,* 12 wheat. 19. One such power is
doubtless the veto power. On the other hand, the President can exercise *only* his constitutional powers, cannot
in other words, in the guise of exercising his discretion,
transcend their limits. Another question relevant to the
general matter under discussion is as to the application
of the doctrine of *stare decisis* in constitutional cases.
There can be no doubt that the doctrine applies in such
cases: Story 1 Comms. §§ 377-8. On the other hand,
however, the doctrine is in nowise necessary to the
theory of judicial review itself. The Supreme Court is
not bound by its own erroneous decisions: *Genessee
Chief* v. *Fitzhugh,* 12 How. 456; the *Legal Tender Cases,*
12 Wall. 457. But the court alone can authoritatively
pronounce its decisions erroneous, and anyone else who
presumes to ignore the precedents does so at his risk.
Also, as said above, executive officers, save where con-
stitutionally vested with a discretion, must follow the

decisions as they find them, and also the acts of the legislature. Such is the nature of the executive office. For
further discussion of the applicability of the doctrine of
stare decisis in constitutional cases, see *Dorr* v. *U. S.*,
195 U. S. 138, 154; 58 Cent. L. J. 29; 3 Harv. Law Rev.
125; 3 Mich. Law Rev. 89, ffg. The argument for judicial review based on the official oath is of course an argument for departmental construction of the constitution.
It was well answered by J. Gibson in his famous dissent
in *Eakin* v. *Raub,* in the following words: "The official
oath . . . relates only to the official conduct of the
officer, and does not prove that he ought to stray from
the path of his ordinary business to search for violations
of duty in the business of others; *nor does it, as supposed,
define the powers of the officer":* 12 Serg. and Rawle
(Pa.) 330, 353. Marshall cites the oath taken by the
judges to uphold the constitution apparently in support of
his contention that the constitution is *law.*

III—The True Meaning of Coke's Dictum: Coke was
what to-day would be called a "political judge"; and it
is possible that there was a period when, the King and
Parliament being at loggerheads and legislation accordingly impossible, he dreamed of giving the law to both.
His final and matured views on the power of Parliament,
however, are those stated in the Fourth Book of his Institutes, in the following passages: "And it is to be known
that the lords in their house have power of judicature
and the commons in their house have power of judicature, and both houses together have power of judicature
(p. 23). . . . Of acts of Parliament, *some be introductory of a new law* [N.B.] and some be declaratory of the
ancient law and some be of both kinds (p. 25). . . . Of
the power and jurisdiction of the Parliament for making
of laws in proceeding by bill, it is so transcendent and
absolute as it cannot be confined either for causes or
persons within any bounds (p. 36). . . . Yet some examples are desired: . . . To attaint a man of treason
after his death. . . . It may bastard a child that by law
is legitimate. . . . To legitimate one that is illegitimate"
(*ib.*). His ideas of "common right and reason" were

therefore not very rigorous. Returning to *Bonham's Case*, we find him citing in support of his dictum a case arising in the manor of Dales, where it was held that an act of Parliament conferring in general terms upon a specific person the jurisdiction of cases arising in the manor did not apply to a case to which that person was an interested party: 8 Rep. 118-20. Judged by this instance all that he means by the word "void," as applied to an act of Parliament, is "inoperative in the particular case when interpreted by Common Law standards." With the dictum should be compared his much later words on p. 37 of the Fourth Book of the Institutes: "I had it of Sir Thos. Gawdye, Knight, a grave and reverend judge of the King's bench, who lived at that time, that Henry VIII commanded him to attend the chief justices and to know whether a man that was forthcoming might be attainted for high treason by Parliament and never called to his answer. The judges answered that it was a dangerous question, and that the High Court of Parliament ought to give examples to inferior courts for proceeding according to justice, and no inferior court could do the like, and they thought that the High Court of Parliament would never do it. But being by the express commandment of the King and pressed by the said earl to give a direct answer, they said that *if he be attainted by Parliament, it could not come in question afterwards,* whether he were called or not to answer. *And albeit their opinion was according to law,* yet might they have made a better answer, for by the statutes of Magna Carta, Cap. 29, 5 Edw. III Cap. 9, and 28 Edw. III Cap. 5, no man ought to be condemned without answer, etc., which they might have certified but *facta tenent multa quae fieri prohibentur; the act of attainder being passed by Parliament did bind, as they resolved."* The position is substantially identical with that afterward taken by Blackstone. See text. See also 4 Mass. 529.

IV—Mingling of Legislative and Judicial Powers: For Parliament's relation to the standing law in the 17th century, see the instructive pages in McIlwain, High Court of Parliament, etc., ch. III, especially pp. 109-66.

Said Harrington in his Oceana: "Wherever the power
of making law is, there only is the power of interpreting
the law so made"; *loc. cit.* 163. See also Blackstone,
I Comms. 160. For the case of the colonial legislatures,
see Works of James Wilson (Andrews' Ed.), II, 50;
Minot, History of Massachusetts, I, 29; Hutchinson,
History of Massachusetts, etc., I, 30, II, 250, 414; 15
Harvard Law Rev. 208-18; Massachusetts Acts and Resolves (to 1780), *passim;* Journal of Virginia House of
Burgesses, *passim.* For the case of the early State legislatures, see Federalist Nos. 48 and 81, the latter of which
is quoted *infra* on this subject. See also Jefferson's
"Virginia Notes" in Works (Mem. Ed.) II, 160-78; also
the Reports of the Pennsylvania Council of Censors of
their sessions of Nov. 10, 1783, and June 1, 1784, in The
Proceedings Relative to the Calling of the Conventions
of 1776 and 1790, etc. (Harrisburg, 1825), pp. 66-128;
also, Tucker's Blackstone, I, app. 81-3, 119-21, 125-6.
See also Langdon of New Hampshire's letters complain-
ing of acts of the State legislature annulling judgments,
in New Hampshire State Papers, XI, 812, 815, and
XXII, 749, 756, (June, 1790). For a concrete case in
N. H., as late as 1791, see the Am. Hist'l Rev. XII, 348-
50, and Prof. W. F. Dodd's remarks concerning it. For
concrete instances in Massachusetts under the constitution of 1780, see Acts and Resolves under following
dates: 1780, May 5, June 9, Sept. 19; 1781, Feb. 12,
Apr. 28, Oct. 10; 1782, Feb. 13, 22, Mar. 5, 7, May 6, 7,
June 7, 18, Sept. 11, Oct. 4, Nov. 2; 1783, Feb. 4, 25;
Mar. 17, Oct. 11; 1784, Feb. 3; 1785, Feb. 28, Mar. 17;
1786, June 27, July 5; 1787, Feb. 26, Mar. 7, July, 7;
1790, Feb. 25, 26, Mar. 9; 1791, Feb. 24. See also *Kil-
ham* v. *Ward et al.,* 2 Mass. 240, 251; also, Proceedings
of the Massachusetts Historical Society, for 1893, p.
231; also Story's Commentaries, § 1367. Further testimony will be found in a speech by Roger Sherman in
his contemporary essays on the Constitution; Moore's
History of North Carolina; Jeremiah Mason's Memories;
Plumer's Life of Wm. Plumer; various judicial his-
tories of Rhode Island, where the practice continued till
1842. The published Index to Rhode Island legislation

to 1842 is immensely instructive in this connection. For
the case of Pa., see Roscoe Pound in 14 Col. Law Rev.
8 (footnote), citing Debates of Pa. Const'l Conv. (1873)
III, 5-20. See also such cases as *Rep.* v. *Buffington,* 1
Dall. 61; *Calder* v. *Bull,* 3 Dall. 386; *Watson* v. *Mercer,*
8 Pet. 88; *Satterlee* v. *Matthewson,* 2 Pet. 380; *Wilkin-
son* v. *Leland, ib.* 657. The overturn of this practice
through a new interpretation of the principle of the
separation of powers is traced *infra.* See also my article
on the Doctrine of Vested Rights in 12 Mich. Law Rev.
247-276.

V—Alleged Precedents for Judicial Review, antedating the Convention of 1787: The *earliest* "precedent"
claimed for judicial review is the Va. case of Josiah
Philips (1778), but the claim is without any basis in
fact. The origin of the claim is to be found in the
following passage on page 293 of the appendix to the
first volume of Tucker's Blackstone (1803): "In May
1778, an act passed in Va. to attaint one Josiah Philips
*unless he should render himself to justice within a limited
time.* He was taken *after the time expired.* and was
brought before the general court to receive sentence of
execution pursuant to the direction of the act. But the
court refused to pass the sentence and he was put upon
his trial according to the ordinary course of law. This
is a decisive proof of the importance of the separation
of the powers of government and of the independence of
the judiciary. A dependent judiciary might have executed the law whilst they execrated the principles upon
which it was founded." Tucker, a zealous champion of
judicial review, is here seeking to create a precedent out
of hand. The myth is elaborated in an ingenious series
of conjectures by Professor W. P. Trent in the Am.
Hist'l Rev. I, 444 ffg. The recollection in the Va. ratifying convention seems to have been that Philips was
executed under the attainder: Elliot III, 66-7, 140,
298-9. This however is wrong. In a letter to Wm. Wirt
of Aug. 15, 1815, Jefferson says: "I remember the case,
and took my part in it. Philips was a mere robber, who
availing himself of the troubles of the times, collected
a banditti, retired to the Dismal Swamp, and from thence

sallied forth, plundering and maltreating the neighboring inhabitants, and covering himself, without authority, under the name of a British subject. Mr. Henry, then governor, communicated the case to me. We both thought the best proceeding would be by bill of attainder, unless he delivered himself up for trial within a given time. Philips was afterwards taken; and Mr. Randolph being Attorney General and apprehending he would plead that he was a British subject, taken in arms in support of his lawful sovereign, and as a prisoner of war entitled to the protection of the law of nations, he thought the safest proceeding would be to indict him as a felon and a robber. Against this, I believe, Philips urged the same plea; but was overruled and found guilty." This letter was communicated to me from the Jefferson MSS. by my friend Mr. W. S. Carpenter, but it or letters to the same effect will be found in Jefferson's published works. In his article entitled A Phantom Precedent, 48 Am. Law Rev. 321-44, Mr. Jesse Turner also brings forward strong evidence to show that, contrary to Tucker's statement that Philips "was taken after the time [set by the act] expired," he was taken before that time. Certainly it is a strange idea that a court would, in 1778, have pronounced a bill of attainder unconstitutional when every legislature in the country was passing such acts, and especially in view of the fact that as late as 1800 the Supreme Court of the U. S. itself held that to pass such acts was within legislative power: 4 Dall. 13.—The *second* "precedent" brought forward for judicial review before the convention of 1787 is the N. J. case of *Holmes* v. *Walton* (1780): Austin Scott in Am. Hist'l Rev. IV, 456 ffg. The case dealt with the question of trial by jury and affords a clear instance of the court's refusing to carry out the will of the legislature on the ground that it transgressed the constitution. The attitude of the court drew forth much unfavorable comment, and though the legislature amended the objectionable act, it met the views of the court only in part. The case is referred to by Gouverneur Morris of Pa. five years later. He did not however, he said, want the judges in Pa. to exercise any such

power: Sparks, Life of Gouverneur Morris, III, 438.
C. J. Brearley of the N. J. court that decided *Holmes* v.
Walton was a member of the Convention of 1787. — The
third "precedent," the Va. case of *Com.* v. *Caton,* 4 Call
5 (1782), is brought forward merely for its *dicta.* Chancellor Wythe and Judge Blair both asserted the right of
the court to resist an unconstitutional act of the legislature, on semi-revolutionary grounds. C. J. Pendleton
was doubtful; see note 54, *supra.* Wythe and Blair
were both members of the Convention of 1787 and Blair
was one of the first bench of the Supreme Court of the
U. S.—The *fourth* "precedent," a municipal court case
from N. Y. City (1783) called *Rutgers* v. *Waddington,*
is urged with even less justification than the Philips case.
It was a marked triumph for the notion of legislative
sovereignty: see my article in 9 Mich. Law Rev. 115-16.
—The *fifth* "precedent" is from Conn., the *Symsbury
Case:* Kirby, 444 ffg. (1785). In this case a legislative
act making a land grant was given a restricted construction so as to prevent its invading a previous grant. The
court invoked fundamental principles, and altogether the
case may be regarded as a somewhat bold application
of Coke's dictum. The decision of the court stood—if
it stood—only because the legislature did not choose to
review it: cf. *Calder* v. *Bull,* 3 Dall. 386.—The *sixth*
"precedent," from N. H., is vouched for by Mr. Meigs
in 47 Am. Law Rev., 684, on the strength of the following passage from Plumer's Life of William Plumer
(p. 59): "I entered my protest singly and alone against
the bill for the recovery of small debts in an expeditious
way and manner, principally on the ground that it was
unconstitutional. The courts so pronounced. it, and the
succeeding legislature repealed the law." These words
were apparently written by Plumer himself of the year
1785 or 1786, but several years later. If this is the case
referred to by Jeremiah Mason in his Memoirs (p. 26),
its claim to be considered a true case of judicial review
is very doubtful. I strongly suspect that this is another instance of precedents made to order. For a true
case of judicial review in N. H. in 1791, invoking the
principle of the separation of powers, see Professor

W. F. Dodd in Am. Hist'l Rev. XII, 348-50.—The *seventh* "precedent" is offered on the strength of a letter by one Cutting to Jefferson in 1788, in which it is asserted that the Mass. court had recently declared an act of the legislature unconstitutional and that the legislature had in consequence repealed the act. A thorough search however fails to reveal any such case or act of repeal: A. C. Goddell, 7 Harv. Law Rev. 415 ffg. The case was probably one in which the court had ruled the act of the legislature involved to be repugnant to the treaty of 1783 with Great Britain. The Mass. legislature had repealed all such acts April 20, 1787, by general description, in conformity with the demand of Congress: See my National Supremacy, ch. III (1913). The only question for the court, therefore, was whether the act before it had been *repealed* or not.—The *eighth* "precedent" is the R. I. case of *Trevett* v. *Weeden*, already referred to. In this case, as Coxe points out, the statute was "repelled," but on the ground allowed by Blackstone, that it was self-contradictory and impossible to be performed, since it required that those violating it be tried *without* a jury but *in accordance with* the "Law of the Land." Nonetheless the case passed as a true constitutional case and met with wide-spread approval: McMaster, History, I, 338 ffg. It is clearly the case that was foremost in the minds of the members of the Convention of 1787 at the opening of the Convention. Far more important than the opinions of the judges was Varnum's argument for defendant, in which the written constitution is thrown about certain fundamental principles of the Common Law and the line is drawn between "legislative" and "judicial" power. To the former alone, Varnum contends, belongs the power of *amending* or *altering* the laws, to the latter *"the sole power of judging of the laws":* see the excerpt from the argument in Haines, p. 90. The argument is given *in extenso* in Coxe.—Finally reference should be made to the early case of *Winthrop* v. *Lechmere* in which, in 1727, the British Privy Coucil "held that an act of the colony of Conn. relating to the division of the property of an intestate among his children was 'null and void as being contrary to the law of the realm, unreasonable, and against the tenor of their character, and consequently the province had no power to make such a law'": Haines, p. 65. Professor Thayer urges truly that this decree was a judicial decree: Cases on Constitutional Law, 39-40. It was argued before the Council as a case at law: see C. M. Andrews in Select Essays in Anglo-Am. Legal Hist., I, 445. But this fact does not make it a precedent for judicial review. The provincial legislatures were in law mere corporations possessed of the powers of legislation of municipal councils. Such bodies to this day, as a general proposition, must not exercise their powers "unreasonably" nor to the transgression of the Common Law: see the following Mass. cases: 3 Pick. 462, 6 *ib*. 187, 11 *ib*. 168, 16 *ib*. 121. The problem of judicial review arises, however, in the first instance, because the legislature was supposed to possess supreme judicial powers, but latterly because of the attribution to the legislature of *sovereignty*. The application of the idea of *sovereignty* to the State legislatures creates an absolutely impossible gulf between such alleged precedents as *Winthrop* v. *Leckmere* and the institution of judicial review in the U. S. Moreover, these cases are *never* referred to by those who developed the argument for judicial review.

VI—The Establishment of Judicial Review in the States: By 1803, the following States had either been definitely committed to the doctrine of judicial review by judicial decision or practically so by judicial dicta: North Carolina (1787), New Hampshire (1791), South Carolina (1792), Virginia (1788, 1793), Pennsylvania (1793, 1799), New Jersey (1796), Kentucky (1801), Maryland (1802). The Kentucky Constitution of 1792, Art. XII. p. 28, says: "All laws contrary . . . to this Constitution shall be void." Prof. Thayer, in his study in 7 Harvard Law Rev., 129 ffg., contended that this article specifically authorized judicial review; but the Pennsylvania constitution of 1776 and the Massachusetts constitution of 1780 contained equivalent provisions without producing judicial review. Of interest in this connection is the opinion of the judges of the Pa. Supreme Court, of

Dec. 22, 1790, to Gov. Mifflin holding that certain offices had been vacated by the new constitution. The ground of the opinion is indicated by the ffg. words: "We think the constitution to be paramount [to] the acts of the legislature": Pa. Archives, 1st Ser., XII, 36. In Pa. however, because of the persistence of the power of the legislature in the matter of private bill legislation, judicial review continued on a precarious basis till a late date. In *Emerick* v. *Harris,* 1 Binn. 418 ffg. (1809), though reference is made to Marshall's argument in *Marbury* v. *Madison,* the court's reliance seems to be chiefly on the duty of the judge by his oath of office and the equality of the judiciary with the other departments, both of which arguments, as we saw above, are quite inadequate. In his famous dissent in *Eakin* v. *Raub,* 12 S. and R. 330 ffg. (1825), Justice Gibson (later chief justice), defining the constitution as an act of *"extraordinary* legislation", and contending that the courts had under it only their Common Law powers of administering the *ordinary* law, rejected judicial review as "a professional dogma," held "rather as a matter of faith than of reason." The power of keeping the legislature within its constitutional bounds, he contended, belonged to the People, its authors. Subsequently as chief justice, Gibson changed his opinion "from experience of the necessity of the case": *Norris* v. *Clymer,* 2 Barr (Pa.) 277, 281. In N. Y., where judicial review was destined to receive its final form, the first judicial claim to the power was made in *Dash* v. *Van Kleeck,* 7 Johns. 477 ffg. (1811). In *Gardner* v. *Newburgh,* 2 Johns. Ch. 162 ffg., five years later, Kent enjoined the enforcement of an act of the legislature on the ground of its invalidity. For the persistence of the idea of judicial review on the basis of fundamental law, apart from the written constitution, see my article in 12 Mich. Law Rev. 247 ffg.; also, C. J. Chase in the License Tax Cases, 5 Wall. 469. The first R. I. case under the constitution of 1842, *Taylor* v. *Place,* 4 R. I. 339, states the doctrine of the separation of powers at length. An interesting Mass. case showing the effect of the doctrine of departmental equality upon judicial logic is that of

Wellington et al., Petitioners, 16 Pick. 87 (1834). Here
we find C. J. Shaw, after first stating the correct doctrine
of judicial review as flowing from the nature of judicial
power in relation to the standing law, then introducing
the notion of three coördinate departments, whereupon
he proceeds as follows (p. 96): "Perhaps . . . it may
well be doubted whether a formal act of legislation can
ever, with strict legal propriety, be said to be void; it
seems more consistent with the nature of the subject
. . . to treat it 'as voidable'." In 24 Pick. 352 (1837),
he abandons this refinement. The history of judicial review in the States may be, generally speaking, divided
into the following periods: 1-1780-87, its tentative suggestion; 2-1787-1800, its rapid advance, under Federalistic influence; 3-1800-1810, its temporary check, under
Jeffersonian influence; 4-1810-1825, its more aggressive
exercise, under the influence of Marshall and Kent and
of the doctrine of "vested rights"; 5-1825-45, its general
recognition, but rare use, on account of the influence of
the Jacksonian Democracy and the rise of the notion of
the "police power"; 6-1845-1857, a period of diversity,
rise of new doctrines of Constitutional Law, conserva-
tism of the N. Y. courts in sharp contrast at the close of
the period to more democratic tendencies in many other
States, protests against "judicial despotism" from certain
courts brought to a climax in criticism of the Dred Scott
decision; 7-1857-1890, judicial review generally used
very moderately, under the influence of the doctrine of
the "police power" as developed by the U. S. Sup. Ct.;
8-1890-1910, a tremendous expansion of judicial review
in all jurisdictions, under the influence of the modern
definitions of "liberty," "property," and "due process of
law"; to-day, reaction in favor of legislative discretion,
under the leadership of the U. S. Sup. Ct. Throughout,
the practice of judicial review in two States, New York
and Massachusetts, has been of leading importance from
the point of view of the history of Constitutional Law,
but the North Carolina, Tennessee, New Hampshire,
Vermont, Pennsylvania, Illinois, and Iowa courts have
also made influential contributions from time to time.
It may be safely said, I think, that more statutes were

invalidated in New York before the Civil War than in any two other States together. On the other hand, in Virginia, where judicial review was at first so strongly asserted, only two acts of the legislature were pronounced void by the court of appeals between 1793 and 1860, and one of these had been repealed some years earlier. During the same period, however, about twenty-five cases were brought before that court in which the constitutional question was raised.

"WE, THE PEOPLE"

"WE, THE PEOPLE"

In the Webster-Hayne debate the South Carolinian set out from the following premises, taken from the Kentucky Resolutions of 1798:

"Resolved that the several States comprising the United States of America . . . by a compact under the style and title of a Constitution for the United States and of amendments thereto . . . constituted a general government for specific purposes, reserving each State to itself the residuary mass of right to its own self-government . . .; that to this compact each State acceded as a State . . .; that as in all other cases of compact among parties having no common judge, each party has an equal right to judge for itself, as well of infractions as of the measures of redress."[1]

This position Webster met with the contention that the Constitution is not a compact among States but,

---

[1] Writings of Thomas Jefferson (Ford Ed.) VII, 289. The third of the Va. resolutions of the same year reads as follows: "Resolved . . . that this assembly doth explicitly and peremptorily declare that it views the powers of the Federal government as resulting from the compact to which the States are parties . . . and that in case of a deliberate, palpable, and dangerous exercise [by the Federal government] of . . . powers not granted by the said compact, the States who are parties thereto, have the right and are in duty bound to interpose for arresting the progress of the evil and for maintaining within their respective limits, the authorities, rights and liberties appertaining to them": Writings of James Madison (Hunt Ed.) VI, 326. Note that Madison does not say that the States are *the* parties (*i. e.* the only parties) to the compact, but simply that they are "parties." This ambiguous position, however, he abandons in his Report of 1799.

by its own declaration, a *law* ordained by the *people*. But, rejoined Calhoun, by what people? and answered: The people of the several States, acting as so many sovereign political communities, since in the first place, it is only a sovereign political community that can enact *law* and since, in the second place, the States were in 1787 the only sovereign political communities on the continent. The Constitution is then, he proceeded, law within the several States by their own ordination, and may be repealed by them at any time, since sovereignty is inalienable. But even before this position was completely thought out, Story had argued in his Commentaries that the language of the Preamble of the Constitution was to be taken literally, and that the Constitution was ordained and established, not by the people of the several States, but by the people of the United States, acting as one people, though within the several States. In his first Inaugural Lincoln adopted this argument and contended further that, far from the States being the only political communities at hand in 1787, the Union was older than the States.

The great historical difficulty in the way of Calhoun's theory of the nature of the Union and the Constitution, once at any rate it is indicated, is obvious enough. It consists in the inversion it effects of the relation between governments and people that is stated by the Declaration of Independence, that all just governments rest on the consent of the governed. Even Calhoun admitted, what indeed would have been undeniable by the hardiest theorizer, that the government of the United States is a government over individuals.[2] Yet he contended that this government did not rest upon the consent of these individuals, but was foisted upon them by the several States. True, the Articles of Confederation rested upon the consent of the States merely, but then, that was not a government over individuals. And the difficulty in question is certainly not lessened by the dogma that inalienable sovereignty was in 1787 a property of the States as political entities. For either this dogma assumes to interpose an absolute veto upon the right of the people to revolutionize their governments or it does not. If

[2] The following is an excellent statement of this principle by Ellsworth in the Connecticut convention: "We see how necessary for union is a coercive principle. No man pretends to the contrary: We all feel and see this necessity. The only question is, shall it be a coercion of law or a coercion of arms? There is no other possible alternative. Where will those who oppose a coercion of law come out? Where will they end? A necessary consequence of their principles is a war of the States one against the other. I am for coercion by law,—that coercion which acts only upon delinquent individuals. This Constitution does not attempt to coerce our sovereign bodies, States, in their political capacity. No coercion is applicable to such bodies but that of an armed force. . . . But this legal coercion singles out the guilty individual and punishes him for breaking the law of the Union": Elliot, II, 197 (The edition used in preparing this article is the Phila. edition of 1881). Ellsworth, however, somewhat exaggerates the immunity of the States from direct control by the National Government. As Madison points out in Federalist No. 39, "In several cases . . . they must be viewed and *proceeded against* in their collective political capacities only": pp. 237-8 (Lodge's Ed.). The contrast between the Confederation as a government over States in their corporate capacities and the government proposed by the Constitution as one over individuals is made with great effect by Hamilton in Fed. No. 15.

it does not, however, then the theory of which the
dogma just recited is an essential part does not effec-
tively contradict the contention that the establishment
of the Constitution of 1787 was an act of popular
revolution; while if it does, it absolutely contradicts
the most fundamental article of the political creed
upon which all American governments are founded.
The truth is that, in the estimation of the men of
1787, the establishment of the Constitution *was* an
act of popular revolution, which not only overturned
the Articles of Confederation, but broke through the
State constitutions also at essential points. The conventions that ratified the Constitution of 1787 were
in no case provided for by the existing State constitutions. In some cases indeed these constitutions for-
bade their alteration or amendment for stated terms
of years. But the adoption of the Constitution of
1787 did nevertheless alter every one of these instru-
ments of government in the most radical fashion.[3]

[3] Note the following passage from the debate of Aug. 31, in
the Convention, touching the method of ratification: "Madison: . . . The people were in fact the fountain of all power,
and by resorting to them all difficulties were got over . . . Mr.
King observed that the constitution of Mass. was made un-
alterable till the year 1790, yet this was no difficulty with him.
The State must have contemplated a recurrence to first principles before they sent deputies to this Convention": Farrand, II,
476-7. See also Madison's words on the floor of the Convention
June 19: "A majority would have the right to bind the rest,
and even to form a new Constitution for the whole." This
idea was brought forward to meet the argument that the Convention had no right to cast the Arts. of Confed. aside, since
they comprised a social compact among the States. But the
idea itself plainly represents Madison's own theory of the
rights of *individuals* under the social compact. Note also Wil-

All this, however, is but introductory. The main purpose of this article is to set forth the most important evidence bearing on the question of the historical validity of the venerable antithesis: The People of the United States vs. the People of the States. This evidence falls into two parts: that drawn from discussions in the State ratifying conventions of the opening phrase of the Constitution, and therefore immediately antedating the establishment of the Constitution; and that drawn from the congressional debates of 1789 on certain propositions of amendment to the Constitution, and therefore immediately subsequent to the establishment of the Constitution. It will be best, I think, to give this evidence first and then the conclusions which it suggests afterward.

I—The evidence from the ratifying conventions, then, is as follows:

King in the Massachusetts convention: "The introduction to this Constitution is in these words: 'We, the people' etc. The language of the Confederation is, 'We, the States' etc. The latter is a mere federal government of States. Those therefore that assemble under it have no power to make laws to apply to the individuals of the States confederated."[4]

son's words on the floor of the Convention, Aug. 30: "We must, in this case [that is the ratification of the Constitution], go to the original powers of society. The house on fire must be extinguished without a scrupulous regard to ordinary rights": Farrand, II, 468-9. *But see especially* the Federalist, Nos. 40, 43, and 45, quoted *infra*.

[4] Elliot, II, 55. Note that the contrast is between *States* and *People,* and that nothing is made of the phrase "of the United States." The same rule holds for the ensuing quotations. I may add here that the evidence given in the text is, to my belief, substantially complete for the State conventions on the subject discussed.

Wilson in the Pennsylvania convention: "In this Constitution all authority is derived from the people. . . . The leading principle in politics and that which pervades the American constitutions is that the supreme power resides in the people. This Constitution . . . opens with a solemn and practical recognition of that principle: 'We the people of the United States, in order etc. do ordain and establish this Constitution for the United States of America'. It is announced in their name—it receives its political existence from their authority. . . . What is the necessary consequence? Those who ordain and establish have the power, if they think proper, to repeal and annul."[5]

And again: "The secret is now disclosed, and it is discovered to be a dread that the boasted State sovereignties will, under this system, be disrobed of part of their power. . . . Upon what principle is it contended that the sovereign power resides in the State governments? The honorable gentleman has said truly that there can be no subordinate sovereignty. Now if there cannot, my position is, that the sovereignty resides in the people; they have not parted with it; they have only dispensed with such portions of power as were conceived necessary for the public welfare. This Constitution stands upon this broad principle. I know very well, sir, that the people have hitherto been shut out of the Federal Government, but it is not meant that they should any longer be dispossessed of their rights. In order to recognize this leading principle, the proposed system sets out with the declaration that its existence depends upon the supreme authority of the people alone. . . . When the principle is once settled that the *people* are the source of authority, the consequence is, that they may take from the subordinate governments powers with which they have hitherto trusted them and placed those powers in the General Government, if it is thought that there they will be productive of good. They can distribute one portion of power to the more contracted circle called State governments. They can

[5] *Ib.* 434-5.

furnish another proportion to the government of the United States."[6]

And again: "The truth is that the supreme, absolute, and uncontrollable authority *remains* with the people. . . . His [Findley's] position is, that the supreme power resides in the States, as governments; and mine is, that it resides in the people, as the fountain of government. . . . I consider the people of the United States as forming one great community; and I consider the people of the different States as forming communities again on a lesser scale. . . . Unless the people are considered in these two views, we shall never be able to understand the principle on which this system was constructed. I view the States as made *for* the people, as well as by them, and not the people as made for the States. The people therefore have a right, whilst enjoying the undeniable powers of society, to form either a general government or State governments, in what manner they please, or to accommodate, them to one another and by this means preserve them all. . . . 'Governments are instituted among men, deriving their just powers from the consent of the governed.' "[7]

And again: "There can be no compact unless there are more parties than one. . . . 'The Convention were forming compacts!' With whom? . . . I am unable to conceive who the parties could be. The State governments make a bargain with one another; that is the doctrine that is endeavored to be established by gentlemen in opposition; their State sovereignties wish to be represented! But far other were the ideas of this Convention, and far other are those conveyed in the system itself."[8]

Henry in the Virginia convention: "What right had

[6] *Ib.* 443-4. Note the equivalent use of the terms *States* and *governments*. Compare Hamilton in Fed. No. 15: "The great and radical vice in the construction of the existing confederation is in the principle of legislation for *States* or *governments,* in their corporate or collective capacities": p. 86 (Lodge).

[7] *Loc. cit.* 456-7.

[8] *Ib.* 497.

they to say 'We the people' . . . instead of 'We the States'? States are the characteristic and soul of a confederation. If the States be not the agents of this compact it must be one great consolidated, national government of the people of all the States. . . . The people gave them no power to use their name. That they exceeded their power is perfectly clear."[9]

And again: "Have they said, We the States? . . . If they had, this would be a confederation. It is otherwise, most clearly, a consolidated government. The question turns, sir, on a poor little thing,—the expression, We the people, instead of the States of America. . . . Here is a resolution as radical as that which separated us from Great Britain."[10]

Randolph in the Virginia convention: "The gentleman then proceeds and inquires why we assumed the language of 'We the people'? I ask, why not? The government is for the people; and the misfortune was that the people had no agency in the government before."[11]

Pendleton in the Virginia convention: "We the people, possessing all power, form a government, such as we think will secure happiness. . . . But an objection is made to the form: the expression, We the people, is thought improper. Permit me to ask the gentleman who made this objection, who but the people can delegate powers? Who but the people have a right to form government? . . . If the objection be, that the Union ought to be not of the people, but of the State governments, then I think the choice of the former very happy and proper."[12]

Lee of Westmoreland in the Virginia convention:' "He [Henry] then adverted to the style of the government and asked what authority they had to use the ex-

[9] Elliot, III, 22-3. Note that Henry, who was opposing adoption, does not find fault with "We, the People of the U. S.," but with "We, the *People*."

[10] *Ib.* 44.

[11] *Ib.* 28.

[12] *Ib.* 35.

pression 'We the people,' and not, We the States. This expression was introduced into that paper with great propriety. This system is submitted to the people for their consideration, because on them it is to operate, if adopted. . . . It is now submitted to the people of Virginia. . . . Suppose it was found proper for our adoption, and becoming the government of the people of Virginia, by what style should it be done?"[13]

Madison in the Virginia convention: "Who are the parties to it? The people—but not the people as composing one great body; but the people as composing thirteen sovereignties. Were it, as the gentleman asserts, a consolidated government, the assent of a majority of the people would be sufficient for its establishment. . . . But, sir, no State is bound by it, as it is, without its own consent. Should all the States adopt it, it will be then a government established by the thirteen States of America, not through the intervention of the legislatures, but by the people at large. . . . The existing system has been derived from the dependent, derivative, authority of the legislatures of the States; whereas this is derived from the superior power of the people."[14]

Corbin in the Virginia convention: "I expected no such objection as this. Ought not the people, sir, to judge of that government whereby they are to be ruled?"[15]

Iredell in the North Carolina convention: The Constitution is not a compact between the rulers and the ruled. This principle is inapplicable "to a government where the people are avowedly the fountain of all power."[16]

Caldwell in the North Carolina convention: "Mr. Chairman, if they mean, *We the people,*—the people at

[13] *Ib.* 42.

[14] *Ib.* 94.

[15] *Ib.* 104.

[16] Elliot, IV, 11. A little later, Iredell added: "We, People, was not to be applied to the members themselves [of the Phila. convention], but was to be the style of the Constitution when it should be ratified in their respective States": *ib.* 23.

large,—I conceive the expression is improper. Were
they who framed this Constitution the representatives
of the legislatures of the different States? In my opinion, they had no power, from the people at large, to use
their name, or to act for them. They were not delegated
for that purpose."[17]

Maclaine in the North Carolina convention: "The
reverend gentleman has told us that the expression, We
the people, is wrong, because the gentlemen who framed
it were not the representatives of the people. I readily
grant that they were delegated by States. But they did
not think that they were the people, but intended it for
the people at a future day. The sanction of the State
legislature was in some degree necessary. It was to be
submitted by the legislatures to the people; so that when
it is adopted, it is the act of the people. When it is the
act of the people, their name is certainly proper. This
is very obvious and plain to any capacity."[18]

Spencer in the North Carolina convention: "The
States do not act in their political capacities, but the
government is proposed for individuals. The very cap-
tion of the Constitution shows that this is the case. The
expression, We the people of the United States, shows
that this government is intended for individuals."[19]

Luther Martin in his Genuine Information: "It is, in
its very introduction, declared to be a compact between
the people of the United States, as individuals; and it is
to be ratified by the *people* at large in their capacity as
individuals; all which . . . would be quite right and
proper if there were no *State governments,* if *all the
people* of this continent were in a *state of nature,* and
we were forming one *national government* for *them as
individuals;* and is nearly the same as was done in most
of the States when they formed their governments *over
the people* who composed them."[20]

Hamilton in Federalist 22: "It has not a little contributed to the infirmities of the existing federal system,

[17] *Ib.* 15-6. Caldwell opposed adoption.
[18] *Ib.* 16.
[19] *Ib.* 153. Spencer opposed adoption.
[20] § 30: Farrand, III, 193. The emphasis is from the original.

that it never had a ratification by the people. Resting on no better foundation than the consent of the several legislatures, it has been exposed to frequent and intricate questions concerning the validity of its powers, and has, in some instances, given birth to the enormous doctrine of a right of legislative repeal. Owing its ratification to the law of a State, it has been contended that the same authority might repeal the law by which it was ratified. However gross a heresy it may be to maintain that a party to a compact has a right to revoke that compact, the doctrine itself has had respectable advocates. The possibility of a question of this nature proves the necessity of laying the foundations of our national government deeper than in the mere sanction of delegated authority. The fabric of American empire ought to rest on the solid basis of THE CONSENT OF THE PEOPLE. The streams of national power ought to flow immediately from that pure, original fountain of all legitimate authority."[21]

Madison in Federalist 39: "It appears, on one hand, that the Constitution is to be founded on the assent and ratification of the people of America, given by deputies elected for the special purpose; but, on the other, that this assent and ratification is to be given by the people, not as individuals composing one entire nation, but as composing the distinct and independent States to which they respectively belong. It is to be the assent and ratification of the several States, derived from the supreme authority in each State,—the authority of the people themselves. The act, therefore, establishing the Constitution, will not be a *national,* but a *federal* act. . . . Were the people regarded in this transaction as forming one nation, the will of the majority of the whole people of the United States would bind the minority, in the same manner as the majority in each State must bind the minority; and the will of the majority must be determined either by a comparison of the individual votes, or by considering the will of the majority of the States as evidence of the will of a

[21] Lodge's edition is used. This and the following passages will be found on pp. 135, 236, 241-2, 246, 275-6.

majority of the people of the United States. Neither of these rules has been adopted. Each State, in ratifying the Constitution, is considered as a sovereign body, independent of all others, and only to be bound by its own voluntary act. In this relation, then, the new Constitution will, if established, be a *federal,* and not a *national* constitution."[22]

Same in Federalist 40: "Let the most scrupulous expositors of delegated powers . . . declare, whether it was of most importance to the happiness of the people of America, that the articles of Confederation should be disregarded, and an adequate government be provided, and the Union preserved; or that an adequate government should be omitted, and the articles of Confederation preserved. . . ." (On the other hand) "let us view the ground on which the Convention stood. . . . They must have reflected, that in all great changes of established governments, forms ought to give way to substance; that a rigid adherence in such cases to the former, would render nominal and nugatory the transcendent and precious right of the people to 'abolish or alter their governments as to them shall seem most likely to effect their safety and happiness'."

Same in Federalist 43: " 'The ratification of the conventions of nine States shall be sufficient for the establishment of this Constitution between the States, ratifying the same.' This article speaks for itself. The

---

[22] *Ib.* p. 236. The advocates of State rights have sometimes ventured to quote portions of this passage in support of their thesis. A careful examination of the terms used however shows that Madison has it in mind to emphasize two points: 1—that the existing States are recognized to the extent that the Constitution, *by its own specific provision,* is to go into effect only in those whose people ratify it; 2—that in the States ratifying it, it will be the act of the *people,* acting as *individuals.* Also, the State rights advocates do not attempt to reconcile their interpretation of Fed. No. 39 with the further language used by Madison in Fed. Nos. 40, 43, and 45, quoted *infra.* See also the passage quoted *infra,* from his Report of 1799.

express authority of the people alone could give due validity to the Constitution. To have required the unanimous ratification of the thirteen States, would have subjected the essential interests of the whole to the caprice or corruption of a single member. It would have marked a want of foresight in the Convention, which our own experience would have rendered inexcusable. Two questions of a very delicate nature present themselves on this occasion: 1. On what principle the Confederation, which stands in the solemn form of a compact among the States, can be superseded without the unanimous consent of the parties to it? 2. What relation is to subsist between the nine or more States ratifying the Constitution, and the remaining few who do not become parties to it? The first question is answered at once by recurring to the absolute necessity of the case; to the great principle of self-preservation; to the transcendent law of nature and of nature's God, which declares that the safety and happiness of society are the objects at which all political institutions aim, and to which all such institutions must be sacrificed."

II—The evidence drawn from the proceedings in Congress in 1789, on the proposed amendments, falls into four groups: 1—Speeches made on Sherman's motion, which was eventually adopted, not to incorporate the proposed amendments in the Constitution, as had been intended by the committee that formulated them, but to append them to it as separate and distinct articles; 2—Speeches made on a proposition, which was eventually lost, to insert in the Preamble of the Constitution a formal declaration of the principle that "governments rest on the consent of the governed"; 3—Speeches made on a proposed amendment, which was also lost, asserting the right of the people to instruct their representatives in Congress; 4—The Tenth Amendment. In no case, of course, are

the speeches quoted below given for their discussion
of the topics immediately in debate, but for the light
they shed upon the historicity of the, today, current
antithesis between "People of the United States" and
"People of the States."

1—From the debate on Sherman's motion:

"Mr. Sherman: If I had looked upon this question as
mere matter of form, I should not have brought it forward or troubled the committee with such a lengthy discussion. But, sir, I contend that amendments made in
the way proposed by the committee are void, . . . I
would desire gentlemen to consider the authorities upon
which the two constitutions are to stand. The original
was established by the people at large, by conventions
chosen by them for the express purpose. The preamble
to the Constitution declares the act: but will it be a truth
in ratifying the next constitution, which is to be done
perhaps by the State Legislatures, and not conventions
chosen for the purpose? Will gentlemen say it is "We
the people" in this case? Certainly they cannot; for, by
the present Constitution, we, nor all the legislatures in
the Union together, do not possess the power of re-
pealing it. All that is granted us by the Fifth Article is,
that whenever we shall think it necessary, we may propose amendments to the Constitution; not that we may
propose to repeal the old, and substitute a new one."[23]

"Mr. Gerry: The honorable gentleman from Connecticut, if I understand him right, says that the words
'We the people' cannot be retained, if Congress should
propose amendments, and they be ratified by the State
legislatures. Now, if this is a fact, we ought most undoubtedly to adopt his motion; because if we do not, we
cannot obtain any amendment whatever. But upon what
ground does the gentleman's position stand? The Constitution of the United States was proposed by a Convention met at Philadelphia; but, with all its importance, it

[23] Annals of Cong., I, col. 742. For the entire proceedings on
the motion, see *ib.*, cols. 734-44, 795.

did not possess as high authority as the President, Senate, and House of Representatives of the Union. For that Convention was not convened in consequence of any express will of the people, but an implied one, through their members in the State legislatures. The Constitution derived no authority from the first Convention; it was concurred in by conventions of the people, and that concurrence armed it with power and invested it with dignity. Now the Congress of the United States are expressly authorized by the sovereign and uncontrollable voice of the people, to propose amendments whenever two-thirds of both Houses shall think fit. Now, if this is the fact, the propositions of amendment will be found to originate with a higher authority than the original system. The conventions of the States, respectively, have agreed for the people, that the State legislatures shall be authorized to decide upon these amendments in the manner of a convention. If these acts of the State legislatures are not good, because they are not specifically instructed by their constituents, neither were the acts calling the first and subsequent conventions."[24]

2—From the debate on the proposed amendment to the Preamble:

"Mr. Tucker replied, that the words 'We the people do ordain and establish this constitution for the United States of America,' were a declaration of their action; this being performed, Congress have nothing to do with it. But if it was necessary to retain the principle, it might come in at some other place."[25]

"Mr. Page thought the Preamble no part of the Constitution; but if it was, it stood in no need of amendment; the words 'We the people,' had the neatness and simplicity, while its expression was the most forcible of any he had ever seen prefixed to any constitution. He did not doubt the truth of the proposition brought for-

[24] *Ib.* cols. 743-4.
[25] *Ib.* col. 745.

ward by the committee, but he doubted its necessity in this place."[26]

"Mr. Madison: If it be a truth, and so self-evident that it cannot be denied; if it be recognised, as is the fact in many of the State constitutions; and if it be desired by three important States, to be added to this, I think they must collectively offer a strong inducement to the mind desirous of promoting harmony, to acquiesce with the report; at least, some strong arguments should be brought forward to show the reason why it is improper."[26]

"Mr. Sherman thought they ought not to come in in this place. The People of the United States have given their reasons for doing a certain act. Here we propose to come in and give them a right to do what they did on motives which appeared to them sufficient to warrant their determination; to let them know that they had a right to exercise a natural and inherent privilege, which they have asserted in a solemn ordination and establishment of the Constitution. Now, if this right is indefeasible, and the people have recognised it in practice, the truth is better asserted than it can be by any words whatever. The words "We the people" in the original Constitution, are as copious and expressive as possible; any addition will only drag out the sentence without illuminating it; for these reasons, it may be hoped the committee will reject the proposed amendment."[26]

3—From the debate on the proposed amendment asserting the right of instruction:

"Mr. Gerry: . . . The friends and patrons of this Constitution have always declared that the sovereignty resides in the people, and that they do not part with it on any occasion; to say the sovereignty vests in the people, and that they have not a right to instruct and control their representatives, is absurd to the last degree. . . ."[27]

[26] *Ib.* col. 746.
[27] *Ib.* col. 765. The entire debate on the subject runs from col. 761 to 776. The motion was rejected by a vote of 41 to 10.

"Mr. Madison: .... The honorable gentleman from Massachusetts asks if the sovereignty is not with the people at large. Does he infer that the people can, in detached bodies, contravene an act established by the whole people? My idea of the sovereignty of the people is, that the people can change the Constitution if they please; but while the Constitution exists, they must conform themselves to its dictates. But I do not believe that the inhabitants of any district can speak the voice of the people; so far from it, their ideas may contradict the sense of the whole people; hence the consequence that instructions are binding on the representative is of a doubtful, if not of a dangerous nature. I do not conceive, therefore, that it is necessary to agree to the proposition now made; so far as any real good is to arise from it, so far that real good is provided for; so far as it is of a doubtful nature, so far it obliges us to run the risk of losing the whole system. . . ."[28]

"Mr. Livermore was not very anxious whether the words were inserted or not, but he had a great deal of doubt on the meaning of this whole amendment; it provides that the people may meet and consult for the common good. Does this mean a part of the people in a township or district, or does it mean the representatives in the State legislatures? If it means the latter, there is no occasion for a provision that the legislature may instruct the members of this body. . . ."[29]

"Mr. Sedgwick opposed the idea of the gentleman from New Hampshire, that the State legislature had the power of instructing the members of this House; he looked upon it as a subordination of the rights of the people to admit such an authority. We stand not here, said he, the representatives of the State legislatures, as under the former Congress, but as the representatives of the great body of the people. The sovereignty, the independence, and the rights of the States are intended to be guarded by the Senate; if we are to be viewed in any other light, the greatest security the people have for their rights and privileges is destroyed. . . ."

[28] *Ib.* col. 767.
[29] *Ib.* col. 770.

[Mr. Livermore said that the gentleman misunderstood him, that what he had said respected only the influence that legislative instructions would have on his private judgment.][30]

"Mr. Page: . . . It was strictly compatible with' the spirit and the nature of the Government; all power vests in the people of the United States; it is, therefore, a Government of the people, a democracy."[31]

4—The Tenth Amendment: "The powers not delegated to the United States *by the Constitution* or prohibited by it to the States are reserved to the *States* respectively, or to the *people.*"[32]

This evidence, drawn as it is from every variety of political opinion contemporary with it, sustains, it is submitted, the following deductions: That in 1787 the terms "People of the States" and "People of the United States" were not antagonistic terms; that the terms opposed by the men of that day were States and People, or more generally Governments and People; that the political science of the day afforded no intermediate term; that governments were universally regarded as properly the creations of the people governed by them; that the States were regarded as respectively the creations of the people politically organized under them; that the term People meant any designated aggregation of individuals endowed with the rights of men under the social compact and especially the right to determine their forms of government; that the Constitution was universally recog-

[30] *Ib.* cols. 771-2.

[31] *Ib.* col. 772.

[32] The antithesis is still between *States* and *people: loc. cit.* col. 797.

nized as proposing a government over individuals; that though the existing organization of the American people into States was recognized to the extent of a specific provision in the Constitution that it was to go into effect only "between the States" ratifying it, as to those States it was to rest upon an act of popular ratification; that the establishment of the Constitution was regarded contemporaneously as representing a fresh manifestation of the inexhaustible, inalienable right of the people to govern themselves.[33]

[33] Further evidence confirming that given in the text is available from the comparison so frequently made of the House of Representatives and the Senate: "The House of Representatives will derive its powers from the people of America. . . . The Senate, on the other hand, will derive its powers from the States, as political and coequal societies": Fed. No. 39, p. 237 (Lodge Ed.). I do not, of course, deny that the Constitution is frequently spoken of as being "ratified by the States," for in colloquial use the term "States" had several meanings: see passage quoted *infra* from Madison's Report of 1799. See also King's language in the Convention, June 19; and again, Johnson's June 29: Gentlemen were using the term "States" in two senses, "those on one side considering the States as districts of people composing one political society; those on the other, considering them as so many societies": Farrand, I, 461. What is insisted upon in the text is, first, that neither the term "of States" nor the term "of United States" added anything in 1787 to the intrinsic force of the term "People"; and secondly, that when used in contradistinction to the term "People," the term "States" signified simply certain governmental creations of the People. The views urged in the text are also supported by the language of *all* the judges in *Chisholm* v. *Ga.* 2 Dall. 419 (1793); by J. Story's language in *Martin* v. *Hunter's Lessee,* 1 Wheat. 304, 324-5 (1816); and by C. J. Marshall's language in *McCulloch* v. *Md.* 4 Wheat. 316, 402-5 (1819). Note particularly the following passage from Marshall's opinion: "It has been said that the people had already surrendered their powers

And from these·conclusions two others necessarily follow: First, that it is a matter of entire indifference, legally speaking, whether the United States was a nation *before* the Constitution was adopted or not, since the Constitution obtains its entire force and efficacy, not from the fact that it was ratified by a pre-existent political community or communities—for it was not—but from the fact that it was established by the people to be governed by it.[33a]   Secondly, that the States have no outstanding rights against the Constitution, that their rights with respect to the Constitution are defined in it, that whether they are in any particular superior to or subordinate to the National Government depends entirely on the terms of the Constitution itself until this is overthrown.   Secession therefore and nullification as alleged constitutional rights go a-glimmering.   The only fundamental outstanding right superior to the Constitution is, in other words, that right of the *people* to the exercise of which it owes its existence, namely, the right of revolution.   Confronted with the question in the Federalist as to what would be the

to the State sovereignties and had nothing more to give. But surely, the question whether they may resume and modify the powers granted to government does not remain to be settled in this country. Much more might the legitimacy of the General Government be doubted had it been created by the States. The powers delegated to the State sovereignties were to be exercised by themselves, not by a distinct and independent sovereignty created by themselves."

[33a] Nor is this to say that the Constitution *made* the U. S. a *nation*. All the factors of nationality were *already* present to the American People save organization under a real government. That, of course, the Constitution supplied for the first time.

consequence if Congress should attempt to usurp
power, Madison answered:. "The same . . . as if
the State legislatures should violate their respective
constitutional authorities," though he further pointed
out, that as a matter of fact, popular resistance to
encroachments upon liberty by the National Government would be easier than resistance to like encroachments by the State governments, since the machinery
of the latter, indispensable as it is at any number of
points to the working of the former, would often-
times be in the hands of the resisters.[34]   And not less
explicit is the answer returned to the same question
by the Virginia ratifying convention.   That body
adopted the following declaration: "We, the delegates of the people of Virginia, . . . do in the name
and in behalf of the people of Virginia declare and
make known that the powers granted under the Constitution being derived from the people of the United
States, may be resumed by them whensoever the same
shall be perverted to their injury or oppression."[35]
To cite this declaration as an assertion of the right of
secession or indeed of any kind of State intervention
is simply absurd.   It is a plain statement of the doctrine of the right of revolution, which is a right not
of governments but of the governed.[35a]

[34] No. 44, p. 283 (Lodge).   See also Nos. 45 and 46; and Hamilton in No. 28.

[35] Elliot, III, 656.

[35a] Said Robert E. Lee, in a letter to his brother, written in
Jan. 1861: "Secession is nothing but revolution. . . . It is idle
to talk of secession.   Anarchy would have been established, and
not a government, by Washington, Hamilton, Jefferson, Madison, and other patriots of the Revolution": Bradford, Lee the

The underlying fallacy of Calhounism is, then, clear once more. It consists in an attempt to appropriate to political entities, called States, rights which properly belong only to populations. As is well known, this fallacy made its first appearance in the Virginia and Kentucky Resolutions of 1798,[36] but it is further illumined by some instructive passages in Madison's famous Report to the Virginia legislature the year following in defence of the Resolutions.

American, p. 35. It is a tenable thesis, I believe, that Calhounism has been more influential with Southern apologists for secession, since the war, than it ever was with the promoters of secession before the war.

[36] It is to be noted, however, that even the Va. and Ky. Resolutions confirm the thesis set forth in the text to this extent, that the State *legislature* is still regarded as the highest organ of the State as a political entity. The intermediate term, in other words, between State, in the sense of government, and the people of the State in their revolutionary capacity, had not yet been found. Madison indeed saw the difficulty that this fact opposed to the doctrine of the resolutions. Thus, on Dec. 29, 1798, he wrote Jefferson thus: "Have you ever considered thoroughly the distinction between the power of the State and that of the legislature on questions relating to the federal pact? On the supposition that the former is clearly the ultimate judge of infractions, it does not follow that the latter is the legitimate organ; especially as the convention was the organ by which the compact was made": Writings (Hunt Ed.) VI, 328 fn. The hint thus given was followed by Calhoun: see *infra*. Madison's discussion of this question throws a curious light on his later attempts to escape the logical consequences of the Resolutions: See letter in Writings, IX, 495 ffg. This was written in Jan. 1833, *after* the Nullification menace had become serious. In his letter to Cabell of Aug. 16, 1829, Madison virtually admits that the difference between South Carolina's doctrine and that of Virginia in 1798 was merely one of degree: *loc cit.*, IX, 343-4.

Reiterating the doctrine that the Constitution is a compact of sovereign States, and for that reason ultimately subject to the construction given it by the States, Madison writes:

"It is indeed true that the term 'States' is sometimes used in a vague sense, and sometimes in different senses, according to the subject to which it is applied. Thus it sometimes means the separate sections of territory occupied by the political societies within each; sometimes the particular governments established by those societies; sometimes those societies as organized into those particular governments; and lastly, it means the people composing those political societies in *their* highest political capacity. . . . In the present instance, whatever different construction of the term 'States' in the resolution *may* have been entertained, all will at least concur in that last mentioned; because in that sense the Constitution was submitted to the 'States'; in that sense the 'States' ratified it; and in that sense of the term 'States' they are consequently parties to the compact from which the powers of the Federal Government result. . . . The Constitution of the United States was formed by the sanction of the States, given by each in *its* sovereign capacity. . . . The States then, being the parties to the constitutional compact, and in *their* sovereign capacity, it follows of necessity that there can be no tribunal above their authority to decide."[37]

In other words, what is at the outset characterized as the highest political capacity of the *people* of the States is finally transmuted by verbal legerdemain into the highest political capacity of the States themselves! The argument reduces itself to a mere pun on the word "States," which is dexterously concealed by an elaborate pretence at definition. Later in the report occurs this sentiment: "The authority of constitu-

[37] Writings, VI, 348-9.

tions over governments and of the sovereignty of the people over constitutions" are truths that cannot be enough emphasized.[38]   Very good.   But if it was the purport of the Resolutions merely to assert the ultimate control of the people of the United States over the Constitution, why all the jargon about "a compact of sovereign States"?   But in the end, as I pointed out in the previous article, Madison abandoned his entire case for State "interposition."

"A declaration," he writes, "that proceedings of the Federal Government are not warranted by the Constitution is a novelty neither among the citizens nor among the legislatures of the States, . . . nor can the declarations of either, whether affirming or denying the constitutionality of measures of the Federal Government, be deemed, in any point of view an assumption of the office of judge.   The declarations in such cases are expressions of opinion, unaccompanied with any other effect than what they may produce on opinion by exciting reflection."[39]

Rather a lame conclusion to so much fulmination! The boasted right of the sovereign State to insert itself between its citizens and the National Government on such occasions as it deemed the latter to be exceeding its powers dangerously comes down in the last analysis to a mere right on the part of its legislature to vote resolutions expressive of opinion, resolutions which are admitted to be no more authoritative than any ebullition of opinion on the part of private citizens.

On the other hand, it must not be concluded that Calhounism is absolutely without justification from

[38] *Ib.* 352.
[39] *Ib.* 402.

the point of view of the history of American political theory. For one thing, even in 1787, there was some difficulty in admitting in the same breath the idea of the Constitution as *law* and the idea of it as a direct act of the people. Government was representative, and until they were unseated, the people's representatives alone had the right to govern, and, therefore, to enact laws.[40] To use the words of Ellsworth on a closely related matter, "a new set of ideas was creeping in." They had not, however, as yet, established themselves so generally but that at this point the Convention of 1787 must be held to have broken with the dominant tradition. But again, while by Calhoun's time, the idea of a constitution as law was well enough established, yet the agency by which constitutions are nowadays drawn up, namely, constitutional conventions, had become such usual phenomena as to have been substantially assimilated to the machinery of *organized government,* so that one looking back to the State conventions that had in 1787 ratified the Constitution found it natural to regard them as organs of existing political societies, rather than as directly representative of the individuals back of those societies. But lastly, Calhounism may be regarded as an effort to restore the somewhat tarnished reputation of the Right of Revolution. A very vital right this was in 1787. Nor was it a merely moral right, for the line between morals and law was as yet but faintly drawn, as evidence of which is the fact that judges themselves claimed power to pass on the validity of laws

[40] See the quotation from Luther Martin's Genuine information immediately below.

under principles of the social compact.[41]   By 1830 however, with the extension of the notion that it was the *sovereignty of the people,* and nothing else, that gave constitutions their legal character, this line had become distinctly delineated and the right of revolution confined to the field of moral rights.   Well, then, some right as good as the right of revolution *had been* must be provided—hence the theory of the right of secession as a *constitutional right.*

But the general subject under discussion has yet another aspect that deserves brief mention.   It is the habit of a certain school of writers nowadays to ring the changes on the assertion that the Convention of 1787 was "undemocratic," and there is undoubtedly some poorly defined truth to the charge.   Nonetheless, this "undemocratic" body made the most audacious and altogether unqualified appeal to the notion of popular sovereignty and majority rule that had ever yet been made, even in America.   For while some of the State constitutions had also been referred for popular ratification by the bodies which formulated them, even these were not at their inception regarded as *law,* while the national Constitution was.

The fact of the matter is, that so far as prerogative and democracy are antagonistic ideas, the opponents of democracy in 1787 were also the opponents of the Constitution.   In this connection let the reader turn to Luther Martin's attack in his Genuine Information[42] upon the supporters of the Constitution for their re-

[41] See the language of Justice Chase in *Calder* v. *Bull,* 3 Dall. 386 (1798).

[42] §§ 104-6, as printed in Volume III of Farrand's Records.

jection of the Articles of Confederation and for the inroads they proposed upon the existing State constitutions, and then to the premises upon which this attack was avowedly based: "Nor do these positions," Martin proceeds,

"in the least interfere with the principle that all power originates from the people, because when once the people have *exercised their power in establishing and forming* themselves into a State government, it never *devolves* back to them, nor have they a *right* to *resume* or *again to exercise that power,* until such events take place as will amount to a *dissolution* of their *State governments.*" The reference of the Constitution to the people, therefore, had "a tendency to set the *State governments* and their *subjects* at *variance* with each other, to lessen the *obligations of government,* to *weaken* the *bonds of society,* to introduce *anarchy* and *confusion* and to *light the torch of discord and civil war* throughout this continent."[43]

This standpat argument was met by Madison in Federalist 45 in the following words:

"Was then," he there inquires, "the American Revolution effected, was the American Confederacy formed, was the precious blood of thousands spilt, and the hard-earned substance of millions lavished, not that the people of America should enjoy peace, liberty, and safety, but that the government of the individual States, that particular municipal establishments, might enjoy a certain extent of power, and be arrayed with certain dignities and attributes of sovereignty? We have heard of the impious doctrine in the Old World, that the people were made for kings, not kings for the people. Is the same doctrine to be revived in the New, in another shape— that the solid happiness of the people is to be sacrificed to the views of political institutions of a different form? It is too early for politicians to presume on our for-

[43] *Ib.* § 106, Farrand, III, 230. The emphasis is from the original.

getting that the public good, the real welfare of the great body of the people, is the supreme object to be pursued; and that no form of government whatever has any other value than as it may be fitted for the attainment of this object. Were the plan of the Convention adverse to the public happiness, my voice would be, Reject the plan. Were the Union itself inconsistent with the public happiness, it would be, Abolish the Union. In like manner, as far as the sovereignty of the States cannot be reconciled to the happiness of the people, the voice of every good citizen must be, Let the former be sacrificed to the latter."

In short, government rests upon the consent of the governed and may be remodelled by them at will to suit their *utility,* all previous governments, states, confederations, constitutions, to the contrary notwithstanding. What more could one demand of the spirit of liberalism in an age when the "social problem" had not yet emerged?[44]

[44] The question at issue between Martin and Madison was really as to the proper scope of the Right of Revolution. Martin's view was that this *right* (not *power*) was available only against *oppression*. Madison and the supporters of the Constitution, on the other hand, took the position that it was available whenever its exercise would prove *beneficial*. This view is undoubtedly sanctioned by the Declaration of Independence, a somewhat radical interpretation of the teachings of which in this reference is that given in a speech by Benj. Hichborn of Boston early in 1777: Civil liberty, said he, was "not a 'government by laws,' made agreeable to charters, bills of rights, or compacts, but a power existing in the people at large, at any time, for any cause, or for no cause but their own sovereign pleasure, to alter or annihilate both the mode and essence of any former government and adopt a new one in its stead": Niles, Principles and Acts, 146-7. Martin's view, however, was the older one. Developing it on the floor of the Convention he had cited in its support Locke, Vattel and others: see Madison's Notes for June 27. Jefferson's idea that there ought to be actual blood-letting about every nineteen years is familiar.

THE PELATIAH WEBSTER MYTH

THE PELATIAH WEBSTER MYTH*

For several years Mr. Hannis Taylor has been endeavoring to persuade the American public that the Constitution, instead of being the work of the Convention of 1787, acting under the guidance of men like Madison, Hamilton, Pinckney, Patterson, Ellsworth, and others of similar caliber, was really the invention of a single individual, Pelatiah Webster by name, whose fame, till Mr. Taylor's resurrection of it in The North American Review for August, 1907, had dropped quite out of historical notice. Since this first publication of his discovery,—I think it was the first,—Mr. Taylor has returned to the attack time and time again, now in a memorial to Congress urging some sort of national recognition of Webster's services, now in a volume on Jurisprudence, again in an imposing work on The Origin and Growth of the American Constitution, and more recently, and compendiously, in the New York *Evening Post* of January 10, 1912, where he attempts to answer Mr. Gaillard Hunt's very pointed criticism in an earlier issue (December 30, 1911) of the same journal, of his method of handling historical evidence in one or two instances. Certainly if asseveration and reiteration could establish the truth of history, Mr. Taylor would by this time have put his thesis beyond all question. But has he in fact succeeded in doing so? This is the subject of our inquiry.

---

* The greater portion of this article appeared in the Michigan Law Review for June, 1912.

First, a word as to the documents involved. For the most part, I shall quote from Mr. Taylor's latest statement of his case, in the *Evening Post* article. But this case in turn is based upon a document. For, as Mr. Taylor reminds us, in the language of M. Langlois: "History is studied from documents. . . . There is no substitute for documents; no documents, no history." Accordingly, between pages 23 and 49 of Mr. Taylor's memorial to Congress, which is available to everybody as Senate Document No. 461 of the 60th Congress, 1st session, will be found, to quote its editor, "the epoch-making document of February 16, 1783, in which is embodied the first draft of the existing Constitution of the United States," the document which entitles its author, Pelatiah Webster, to be regarded as "the architect of our Federal Constitution." Further along Mr. Taylor adds: "Strange indeed it is that the most important document connected with our constitutional history should now be presented to the jurists and statesmen of the United States as if it were a papyrus from Egypt or Herculaneum."

Sketched in outline, Mr. Taylor's case for Webster is as follows: The United States is a federal government, but a federal government of a unique sort, in that it operates directly upon the individuals subject to it instead of through the governmental machinery of its component States. Originally the United States, as organized under the Articles of Confederation, was itself of the usual type of federal government, being dependent even for its revenue upon State action. This system, however, soon proved inadequate, and

particularly on its financial side.   Now as it chanced,
Pelatiah Webster of Philadelphia was a student of
finance.   Approaching the subject of the deficiencies
of the Confederation from the angle afforded by his
favorite studies, Webster was able to make an almost
unparalleled contribution to the science of government.
The system of State requisitions had failed.   The
central government must therefore have a revenue of
its own, to be levied by its own legislature and to be
collected by its own agents.   For financial purposes at
least, then, the central government must act *directly*
on the people, and not *indirectly* through the States.
Thus at one leap was the tremendous barrier that de-
marks the American system from all other federal
systems surmounted.   For this great feat achieved, all
the rest was easy enough for the mind that had
achieved it.   Not only was Webster the first to sug-
gest a federal *revenue,* but he was the first to outline
the entire system embodied in the Constitution of 1787.

But now is it true that Webster *was* the first to propose that the Federal Government should have "the
independent power to tax," that before him "no one
had dreamed of a federal state with the independent
power of taxation," that this proposition "made all
possible," involving "the creating of a distinct and
self-sustaining federal government such as had never
existed"?

Webster's proposition to invest "the supreme
authority" of the Union with "power of taxation,"
meaning by that the power to levy import duties,
which he urged should be particularly heavy upon

articles "consumed by the rich or prodigal part of the
community," occurs on page 26 of Senate Document
Number 461. *On that very page* Webster himself
refers to the recent action of Rhode Island in rejecting
an amendment to the Articles of Confederation by
which Congress was to be given the power to levy a
5 per cent import duty! This amendment was first
proposed in February, 1781, and so antedates Webster's pamphlet an even two years. Even earlier was
Hamilton's famous letter of September 3, 1780, to
James Duane urging a "solid coercive union," a powerful executive consisting of few heads, a federal revenue, a tax in kind, and a national bank. Mr. Taylor is
quite aware of this letter of Hamilton's but sets it down
as of "no importance" on account of its alleged private
character. "It was not a public act, not even a public
declaration," he says. But is this a valid line of argument? The letter, whether it be regarded as *public*
or *private,* still comprises an index to its author's general interests and conversation, as well as of the group
in which he moved. This is proved by the very sentence with which it opens: *"Agreeably to your request and my promise,* I sit down to give you my
ideas of the defects of the present system and the
changes necessary to save us from ruin." But the fact
is that the letter was, in a very true sense of the term,
a *public* one, though it was not at the time *published*
through the press. Its author was the private secretary of the Commander-in-chief of the Continental
Army. Its recipient was a member of Congress. The
topic it dealt with was one of public interest. Its

dimensions were those of a pamphlet. Finally, one of the specific proposals contained in it resulted in the plan from the congressional committee of which Duane was a member, establishing a Department of Foreign Affairs with a Secretary. This occurred in January 1781, many months before Webster had conceived his pamphlet.[1]

But indeed, not even Hamilton is entitled to the credit of *first* suggesting, the idea of a federal system the central authority of which should be vested with an independent power of taxation. More than a quarter of a century before the letter to Duane was written, three years before its author had yet seen the light of day, Benjamin Franklin had proposed a federal government for the British Colonies of North America, "for their mutual defense and security." This was the so-called "Albany Plan of Union" of 1754. The governing body of the Union was to be a "Grand Council" composed of forty-eight members, apportioned among the colonies in a way to recognize, to some extent, their relative population and importance. But the central feature of the scheme was the grant of power to the Grand Council. They were to regulate all trade with the Indians, to make new settlements, to govern these till the crown should

[1] For the Duane letter, see Writings of Alexander Hamilton (Lodge, Ed.) I, 213 ffg. It is worth noting, in view of Mr. Taylor's insistence on the importance of the printed word that Hamilton did in fact *publish* a series of papers in one of which, bearing date of Aug. 30, 1787, he repeated his recommendation of a tax to be "granted to the Federal Government in perpetuity, and, if Congress think proper, to be levied by its own collectors": 25 Harv. Law Rev. 748.

"form them into particular governments," to "raise and pay soldiers," "build forts," "equip vessels of force to guard the coast and protect the trade on the ocean, lakes, or great rivers," and for these purposes, to

"have the power to make laws and *lay and levy such general duties, imports, or taxes, as to them shall appear most equal and just, considering the ability and other circumstances of the inhabitants in the several colonies, and such as may be collected with the least inconvenience to the people, rather discouraging luxury, than loading industry with unnecessary burdens.*"

It is true that the Plan does not state specifically whether the collectors of the federal revenue were to be appointed by the Grand Council or the colonial governments, but at least the intervention of the colonial legislatures in the *levying* of federal taxes, which was the major cause of the failure of the Articles of Confederation, was avoided.[1a]

But not only does the Albany Plan, to this extent at least, anticipate both Hamilton and Webster in their suggestion of a federal government with an independent revenue, but it also suggests the question whether Mr. Taylor has not exaggerated somewhat the difficulty in the way, in the year 1783, of conceiving of a federal government acting upon individuals. In this connection the testimony of Madison in the Federalist is most instructive and it is, moreover, testimony which must be very persuasive with Mr. Taylor. Thus writing in Federalist 40, Madison compares the scheme

[1a] For the Albany Plan, see Wm. MacDonald, Select Charters, 253 ffg. See also Mrs. Lois K. Matthews' interesting study in The Am. Polit'l Sc. Rev., VIII, 393 ffg.

proposed by the new Constitution with that organized
by the Articles of Confederation thus:

"In some instances, as has been shown, the powers of
the new government will act on the States in their collective characters. In some instances, also, those of the
existing government act immediately on individuals. In
cases of capture, of piracy, of the post-office, of coins,
weights, and measures, of trade with the Indians, of
claims under grants of land by different States, and,
above all, in the case of trials by court-martial in the
army and navy, by which death may be inflicted without
the intervention of a jury, or even of a civil magistrate;—
in all these cases, the powers of the Confederation operate immediately on the persons and interests of
individual citizens. . . . The truth is, that the great
principles of the Constitution proposed by the Convention may be considered less as absolutely new, than as
the expansion of principles which are found in the
Articles of Confederation."

Yet Madison himself admits in the end that "the
new system" had "the aspect of an entire transforma-
tion of the old," so that the question of originality is
still before us, even though in tones somewhat sub-
dued. Also, it must be conceded that, while Webster
was plainly no pioneer in urging an import duty for
the government of the Confederation, he may still
have been the originator of other not less important
features of the Constitution of 1787. In other words,
it is possible that, while Mr. Taylor is mistaken as to
the exact road by which Webster approached the great
discoveries in government attributed to him, he may
still be right in crediting him with those discoveries.
We thus return to Mr. Taylor's claims for his hero,
with a view to comparing them with the hero's actual
performance.

Mr. Taylor's second claim for Webster is, then, that he first proposed the extension to the Federal Government of the principle of checks and balances and the separation of powers. His language is as follows: "No one had dreamed of a federal legislature divided into two chambers; no one had dreamed of a federal state divided into three departments; executive, legislative and judicial."

The answer to this claim is twofold. In the first place, what Mr. Taylor asserts "no one had dreamed of," had been apparently a matter of discussion and deliberation, and that at the very foundation of the Union. Ultimately however, John Adams informs us, the principle of the separation of powers was not extended to "the United States in their federal capacity," because "the people of America and their delegates in Congress were of opinion that a single assembly was in every way adequate to the management of all their federal concerns"; and he adds that this was a reasonable decision, "because Congress is not a legislative assembly . . . but only a diplomatic assembly."[2] But now, it is worth noting, as bearing on the whole question of Webster's merits as a political thinker, that, while he did indeed propose to divide Congress into two houses,[3] it never occurred to him to touch the real source of mischief, namely Congress's appointment by and responsibility to the States. In other words, Congress is still to remain a diplomatic assembly in which the States shall be represented, precisely as under the Articles of Confederation, by delegates "appointed by

[2] Life and Works IV, 579. See also *ib*. 208.
[3] Senate Document No. 461, 60th Congress, p. 33.

the States in any manner they please" and subject to recall by the States "as often as they please."[4]

But in the second place, aside from this anomalous proposition to divide a diplomatic body into two chambers, which, in the case of their being unable to agree in the face of a crisis, were to bestow all their powers upon a dictator after the Roman model,[5] Webster had not the faintest idea of applying the principle of checks and balances to the Federal Government. True, like Hamilton before him, he would have a collegiate executive, a "Council of State," but this council was to be appointed, certainly in part, probably in entirety, by Congress,[6] to which moreover "all and singular of them" were to be "ever accountable." As to the part that this council was to have in legislation, Webster writes thus: *"I do not mean to give these great ministers of State a negative on Congress,* but I mean to oblige Congress to receive their advices before they pass their bills, and that every act shall be void that is not passed with these forms."[7] In view of this very specific language how remarkable that Mr. Taylor should write thus: "Under Webster's plan, *now in force,* federal legislation is enacted by three bodies— the executive, the House of Representatives and the Senate. The President of the United States is a part of the law-making power. *That is what Webster said, no more, no less"!*

But Mr. Taylor's third claim in his hero's behalf is

[4] *Ib.* p. 27.
[5] *Ib.* p. 42.
[6] *Ib.* p. 43.
[7] *Ib.* p. 37.

even more preposterous. Stated in his own language it runs thus: "He outlined the Supreme Court with jurisdiction both original and appellate," he anticipated "the splendid conception of the Supreme Court as it now exists," he "provided for the complete supremacy of federal law" and "paved the way for Marshall's great judgment in *Cohens* v. *Virginia.*"

What is the basis for these sweeping assertions? It is supplied by the following passage from Webster's pamphlet: "That the supreme authority should be vested with powers to terminate and finally decide controversies arising between different States, I take it, will be universally admitted, but I humbly apprehend that an appeal from the first instance of trial ought to be admitted in causes of great moment, on the same reasons that such appeals are admitted in all the states of Europe."[8]

The important point to be made clear in this reference is the meaning of the term "the supreme authority." Obviously, it is the same "supreme authority" for which already Webster has urged the right to levy a customs duty[9]; again it is the same "supreme authority" for which in the paragraph immediately following the one just quoted from he claims the, "power of peace and war, and forming treaties": it is, in short, *Congress.*[10] But also, it should be observed, Webster himself claims no credit for originality in urging that Congress should have power to terminate "controversies arising between different

[8] *Ib.* p. 31.
[9] *Ib.* p. 26.
[10] *Ib.* p. 33.

States," and his modesty in this respect is most becoming, since by Article IX of the Articles of Confederation, Congress was already possessed of this power. Yet it is certain that the Articles of Confederation did not produce a *Cohens* v. *Virginia*.

But not only would Mr. Taylor have it that Webster proposed the Supreme Court with its present jurisdiction, but also that he prevised the entire federal judicial system. Thus on page 18 of the memorial to Congress he writes as follows: "After an elaborate discussion of the qualifications of members of Congress . . . he proceeded to define a part of the original jurisdiction of the Supreme Court of the United States by saying 'that the supreme authority should be vested with power to terminate and finally decide controversies between different States.' He also said 'to these I would add judges of law and chancery.' Thus the entire federal judicial system was distinctly outlined."

Mr. Taylor's endeavor to identify Webster's "supreme authority" with the present Supreme Court has been already disposed of. Our interest at this point is in the second one of the sentences just quoted. What is the significance of the word "these" in this sentence, to whom does it refer? Mr. Taylor's obvious intention is to convey the impression that it refers to the "supreme authority," that is, as *he* would have it, the Supreme Court. As a matter of fact, however, when we turn to Webster's pamphlet we find "these" separated from the antecedent which Mr. Taylor provides for it by more than five pages,[11] and

[11] *Ib*. pp. 31 and 36.

that the antecedent which Webster supplies has nothing to do with the "supreme authority," but refers to
those Ministers of State who were to constitute his
council of legislative revision. "To these," he writes,
"I would add judges of law and chancery, but I fear
they will not be very soon appointed." In other
words, the very sentence from which Mr. Taylor presumes to quote in support of his proposition that
Webster foresaw the federal judicial system, proves
precisely the contrary.

And with Webster's federal judiciary thus vanish-
ing in the thin air of illusion, what becomes of the
further claim that he conceived the idea of a "supreme
law of the land" enforceable by that judiciary? The
fact is of course that Webster never even distantly
approached such a conception. It is true that he
would give the "supreme authority" "sufficient powers
to enforce the obedience of all subjects of the United
States" to its treaties[12] and "to punish all transgressors
in all these respects,"[13] but what is the method he
relies upon for making good these powers of enforcement? He sets it forth on page 45 of the published
pamphlet thus: "I therefore propose, that every person whatever, whether in public or private character,
who shall, by public vote or overt act, disobey the supreme authority, shall be amenable to Congress, shall
be summoned and compelled to appear before Congress, and, on due conviction, suffer such fine, impris-
onment, or other punishment, as the supreme authority
shall judge requisite." This, from "the Architect of

[12] *Ib.* p. 31.
[13] *Ib.* p. 32.

the Federal Constitution," who, according to Mr. Taylor, "proposed the division of a Federal State into three departments, executive, legislative, and judicial, *the organization of each of which he worked out"!*

However, we must look at this proposition of Webster's from another point of view, namely, as a proposal to make the federal power operative upon individuals, without the intervention of the States, which, according to Mr. Taylor, was yet another, indeed the most important of Webster's discoveries. Thus, in his letter memorializing Congress "in behalf of the Architect of our Federal Constitution," Mr. Taylor writes: "Having thus defined his fundamental concept of a federal government *operating directly on the citizen,* the great one boldly accepted the inevitable corollary that such a government must be strictly organized and equipped with . . . all the usual apparatus of a government, *all bearing directly upon every citizen of the United States without any reference to the government of the several States."*[14] But now what is the fact of the matter? It is that Webster had not the least idea of dispensing with the State governments as the *usual* intermediaries between the government of the Union and its subjects. Thus, while vesting Congress with a customs revenue, he still retains State requisitions.[15] Again, his notion of hailing persons before Congress for transgressing the acts of the Union is devised principally, it seems plain, with the idea of punishing members of the State legislatures for voting measures opposed to the "supreme

[14] *Ib.* p. 16.
[15] *Ib.* pp. 30, 43.

authority." But finally, it is upon State coercion that he relies principally for securing the authority of the Federal Government. Thus he writes: "There remains one very important article still to be discussed, namely, what methods the Constitution shall point out to enforce the acts and requisitions *through the several States; and how the States which refuse or delay obedience to such acts and requisitions shall be treated.*" And again: "to leave all the *States* at liberty to obey" the acts of Congress "or not with impunity, is, in every view, the grossest absurdity." And again: "every *State* in the Union is under the highest obligation to obey the supreme authority of the whole." And again: "I cannot therefore admit, that the great ends of our Union shall lie at the mercy of a single *State,* or that the energy of our government should be checked by a single disobedience." What he proposed, accordingly, was this: first, that any State might petition Congress for the repeal of any law or decision, and that if a majority of the States did so propose, the law or decision in question should be repealed, but secondly, that "if the execution of any act or order of the supreme authority shall be opposed by force in any of the States . . . it shall be lawful for Congress to send into such State a sufficient force to suppress it."[16]

In other words, under Webster's scheme, as under the Articles of Confederation, the States still remained the essential units of the Federal Government. and the supremacy of the federal authority was to be

[16] *Ib.* pp. 43-7.

secured by State coercion. But with reference to
State coercion, there are just these two facts to be re-
membered: first, that the idea was not original with
Webster, having been proposed as early as March
1781, by a committee of Congress itself, the spokes-
man of which was Madison; secondly, that the idea
was utterly repudiated by the Convention that framed
the Constitution, as impracticable and destructive and,
under the system before the Convention, unnecessary.
And yet Mr. Taylor asserts that Webster's pamphlet
furnished the Convention of 1787 "the basis of its
proceedings"!

One point further. In his recent book on The Origin and Growth of the American Constitution, as
earlier, Mr. Taylor has endeavored to secure for Webster the credit for a pamphlet written in 1781 in which,
Hamilton's letter to Duane aside, the proposition of a
continental convention for the purpose of enlarging
the powers of Congress was first broached. Mr.
Taylor bases this claim upon the testimony of Madison, given late in life. This testimony, however, the
historian Bancroft specifically rejects: first, because,
when at a later period Webster collected his pamphlets
in a volume, he did not include the pamphlet in question; secondly, because the style of the pamphlet is
totally unlike that of the rest of Webster's writings;
thirdly, because the bill for the printing of the
pamphlet was made out to one William Barton;
fourthly, because "Barton from time to time wrote
pamphlets, of which on a careful comparison, the style,
language and forms of expression are found to corre-
spond to this pamphlet published in 1781." Notwith-

standing this convincing array of reasons, Mr. Taylor has the hardihood in a footnote[17] to write thus: "No attention should be paid to Bancroft's vain attempt to discredit Madison's statement . . . Madison was on the ground and knew the facts; Bancroft's inference is based on flimsy hearsay nearly a century after the event"!

Altogether, it becomes quite clear that Mr. Taylor's efforts to enroll Pelatiah Webster with the world's great lawgivers have failed,—although, of course, one could never predict what a cipher might yet reveal! But indeed Mr. Taylor should have better assessed the difficulties of his enterprise. For while rural churchyards may now and then shelter "some mute, inglorious Milton," it seems most unlikely that a period in which both the minds of men and the printing press fairly teemed with schemes of constitutional reform,—when politics was *the* intellectual interest,— would have relegated a really superior thinker along these lines to an undeserved oblivion. Rather it would have provided genius with platform and pedestal—as in truth it did in the case of both Hamilton and Madison. The author of the pamphlet of February 16, 1783, was, however, no genius. Madison, on the basis of his recollection of him, even hesitated to credit him with ability. For having described him as "an able citizen of Philadelphia," he later struck out the adjective. No doubt to have been a citizen of Philadelphia was not without merit, but after all, it hardly entitles one of itself to a place with Moses and Lycurgus.

[17] See The Origin and Growth of the American Constitution, p. 27.

THE DRED SCOTT DECISION

THE DRED SCOTT DECISION[1]

The purpose of the following study is to consider the Dred Scott decision[2] in the light of legal doctrine contemporary with it, in the view particularly of reassessing the pronouncement therein of unconstitutionality upon the Missouri Compromise.[3]

I

The main facts leading up to and attending this famous case may be summarized as follows:[4] Dred, a slave belonging to an army officer named Emerson, was taken by his master from the home State, Missouri, first into the free State of Illinois and thence into that portion of the national territory in which, by the eighth section of the Missouri Compromise, slavery had been "forever prohibited." Here master and slave remained two years before returning to Missouri, the latter in the meantime marrying with his master's consent. In 1852 Dred sued his master for

[1] In substance this paper was read before the American Historical Association at its annual meeting of December, 1910, and was later published in more extended form in the Am. Hist'l Rev., XVII, No. 1.

[2] 19 Howard 393-633 (cited below as "Rep.").

[3] For the conventional view of *Scott* v. *Sanford*, see James Ford Rhodes, History of the United States, II, 251 ffg.; James Schouler, History of the United States, V. 377 ffg.; Nicolay and Hay, Abraham Lincoln, II., ch. 4; Theodore Clarke Smith, Parties and Slavery, ch. 14.

[4] The agreed statement of facts is to be found, Rep. 397-399.

freedom in one of the lower State courts and won the action, but upon appeal the decision was reversed by the supreme court of the State, upon the ground that appellee's status at home was fixed by State law regardless of what it had been abroad—a decision which plainly ran counter to the whole trend of decision by the same court for the previous generation. Thereupon the case was remanded to the inferior court for retrial, but Dred, having in the meantime become the property of one Sanford, a citizen of New York, now decided to bring a totally new action in the United States circuit court for the Missouri district, under section 11 of the Act of 1789. In order to bring this action Dred had of course to aver his citizenship of Missouri, which averment was traversed by his adversary in what is known as a plea in abatement, denying the jurisdiction of the court upon the ground that plaintiff was the descendant of African slaves and had been born in slavery. The plea in abatement the circuit court overruled, but then proceeded to find the law on the merits of the case for the defendant; and from this decision Dred appealed to the United States Supreme Court.

Scott v. *Sanford* was first argued before the Supreme Court in the December term of 1855. From a letter of Justice Curtis we learn that in the view the court then took of the case, it would find it unnecessary to canvass the question of the constitutionality of the Missouri Compromise.[5] And indeed it was evidently of a mind to evade even the question of juris-

[5] Curtis to Ticknor, April 8, 1856: George Ticknor Curtis, Life of Benjamin Robbins Curtis, I, 80.

diction, had it not been for the fact, as it presently developed, that Justice McLean, who aspired to the Republican presidential nomination, had determined to make political capital of the controversy by writing a dissenting opinion, reviewing at length the history of African slavery in the United States from the Free Soil point of view.[6] McLean's intention naturally produced some uneasiness among his brethren and particularly such as came from slave States, three of whom now began demanding reargument of the questions raised by the plea in abatement. This demand being acceded to, the case came on for reargument in the December term of 1856, that is, after the presidential election was past. Yet even now it was originally the purpose of the court to confine its attention to the question of law raised by the circuit court's decision, which rested upon the same ground as the State supreme court's earlier decision, and Justice Nelson was commissioned to write an opinion sustaining the circuit court.[7]

[6] Ashley of Ohio's positive testimony, on the basis of report current at the time *Scott* v. *Sanford* was pending, supplies the explanation needed of the demand for reargument, since the final disposition of the case would be precisely the same whether the circuit court were held to have erred in taking jurisdiction or, having rightfully taken jurisdiction, to have properly decided the case on its merits: Congressional Globe, 40th Cong., 3d sess., App., p. 211. Ashley's testimony is moreover confirmed by that of Justice Grier in the letter cited below in note 9. See also McLean's opinion, Rep. 529-564, and Curtis's animadversions on the same, *ib.*, 620.

[7] Rep. 529-564. The fact that Nelson was commissioned to write an opinion *sustaining* the lower court again shows that intrinsically the question of the lower court's jurisdiction was regarded as unimportant.

But with the defeat of Fremont, and Buchanan's election, the advantage of position now lay with the pro-slavery contingent of the court. Two of this group, accordingly, Wayne of Georgia and Catron of Tennessee, soon began urging the notion that, as expressed in Wayne's very frank opinion, "the peace and harmony of the country required the settlement . . . by judicial decision" of the "constitutional principles" involved in the case.[8] From Daniel of Virginia and Campbell of Georgia, the two agitators apparently encountered little opposition; indeed, their well-founded apprehension seems to have been that these two justices would seize the occasion to "throw out" "some extreme views." The aged Chief Justice proved at first more difficult, but he too at last yielded and consented to write what in the Report is absurdly labelled "the Opinion of the Court," covering all issues that had been raised by counsel's argument. It now only remained to align one of the Northern justices with the majority, since otherwise the sectional and partisan character of the decision would appear too palpable. On February 19, 1857, Catron, whose own efforts to this end had thus far proved unavailing, appealed to the President-elect to persuade his fellow Pennsylvanian, Grier, to join "the majority of his brethren" in a broad gauge decision of the entire question of Congress' power in the territories, instead of taking, as he seemed disposed to do, "the smooth handle for the sake of repose." Buchanan, at once wrote Grier as he was bid, and Grier promptly responded with the

8 Rep. 454-5.

desired promise. In his inaugural address, a few days later, Buchanan, again taking his orders from Catron, referred to the pending decision, indicated the scope it would take, and bespoke the acquiescence of all good citizens in it, "whatever it might be"![9]

II

Hostile criticism of the Dred Scott decision, naturally, has always found its principal target in the Chief Justice's opinion, and the gravamen of such criticism has always been that the portion of it dealing with the Missouri Compromise, was *obiter dictum*. I do not, however, concur with this criticism, for reasons which I shall now endeavor to make plain.

To begin with, it ought to be clearly apprehended what difficulty attaches to a charge of this sort against a deliberate utterance of the Supreme Court of the United States, evidently intended by it to have the force and operation of law, and for the reason that the ultimate test of what *is* law for the United States is, and at the time of the Dred Scott decision was, the opinion of the Supreme Court. On the other hand, the Supreme Court is not a legally irresponsible body: by the very theory that makes it final judge of the laws and the Constitution it is bound by these; as by virtue

[9] Catron's and Grier's letters will be found in the Works of James Buchanan (J. B. Moore Ed.) X, 106-8 fn. Grier's answer of Feb. 23 to Buchanan's note gave the President-elect complete information as to the alignment of the Court. A. H. Stephens was aware of the scope the decision was to take as early as Jan. 1857: Rhodes, II, 253. And to know the scope of the decision was, in view of the make-up of the court, to know its purport.

of its character as *court* it is bound by the *lex curiae*, that is to say, is bound to make consistent application of the results of its own reasoning, and to honor the precedents of its own creation unless it is able to stigmatize them as erroneous. What the charge of *obiter dictum* amounts to then is this: first, that the action of the Chief Justice in passing upon the constitutionality of the eighth section of the Missouri Compromise was *illogical,* as being inconsistent with the earlier part of his opinion, the purport of which, it is alleged, was to remove from the court's consideration the record of the case in the lower court and, with it, any basis for a pronouncement upon the constitutional question; and secondly, that it was *in disregard of precedent,* which, it is contended, exacted that the court should not pass upon issues other than those its decision of which was strictly necessary to the determination of the case before it, and particularly that it should not unnecessarily pronounce a legislative enactment unconstitutional. Let us consider these two points in order.

As already indicated, the primary question before the court upon the reargument was what disposition to make of the plea in abatement which the circuit court had overruled, thereby taking jurisdiction of the case,[10] and upon this point a majority of the court, including both Chief Justice Taney and Justice Curtis, ruled decisively both that the plea in abatement was before it and that the decision of the circuit court as to its jurisdiction was subject to review by the Su-

[10] Supreme Court Reports, Lawyer's Edition, Bk. xv., 694, 697.

preme Court.[11]   Evidently the charge of illogicality
lies against only those judges of the above-mentioned
majority who, after sustaining the plea in abatement
and so pronouncing against the jurisdiction of the
circuit court upon the grounds therein set forth, passed
to consider the further record of the case, by which
the constitutional issue was raised.   But *was* such proceeding necessarily illogical?   Upon this point obviously the pertinent thing is to consider Taney's own
theory of what he was doing, which he states in substantially the following language at the conclusion of
his argument on the question of plaintiff's citizenship: But waiving, he says, the question as to whether
the plea in abatement is before the court on the writ
of error, yet the question of jurisdiction still remains
on the face of the bill of exceptions taken by plaintiff in which he admits that he was born a slave
but contends that he has since become free; for if he
has not become free, "he is still a slave and certainly
incapable of suing in the character of a citizen."[12]   In
other words, the Chief Justice's theory was, not that
he was canvassing the case on its merits, which he
could have done with propriety only had he chosen to
ignore the question of jurisdiction, but that he was

[11] This majority consisted of the Chief Justice and Justices
Wayne, Daniel, Campbell, and Curtis.   Grier considered it
sufficient to canvass the question of the lower court's jurisdiction
on the basis of the facts stated in the bill of exceptions.   Nelson
did not consider the question of jurisdiction.   Catron and
McLean did not deem the question of jurisdiction to be before
the court.

[12] Rep. 427.   Note also the Chief Justice's statement of the
issue at the opening of his opinion, Rep. 400.

fortifying his decision upon this matter of jurisdiction by reviewing the issues raised in the bill of exceptions, *as well as* those raised by the plea in abatement; in other words that he was canvassing the matter of jurisdiction afresh.

The question of the validity of the Chief Justice's way of proceeding then comes down to this question: Is it allowable for a court to base a decision upon more than one ground and if it does so, does the auxiliary part of the decision become *obiter dictum?* On the general question of what constitutes *dictum* we find the writer in the American and English Encyclopedia of Law indicating the existence of two views among Common Law courts. By one of these views none of a judicial opinion is decision save only such part as was absolutely necessary to the determination of the rights of the parties to the action. By the other view, on the contrary, *all* of an opinion is decision which represents a deliberate application of the judicial mind to questions legitimately raised in argument.[13] But on the precise question just stated the above-mentioned writer speaks as follows:

"Where the record presents two or more points, any one of which, if sustained, would determine the case, and the court decides them all, the decision upon any one of the points cannot be regarded as *obiter*. Nor can it be said that a case is not authority on a point because, though that point was properly presented and decided in the regular course of the consideration of the case, another point was found in the end which disposed of the whole matter. The decision on such a question is as

[13] Encyc. (2d ed.), "Dictum," IX, 452-453; "Stare Decisis," XXVI, 168-169. *Cf. Carroll* v. *Carroll's Lessee,* 16 How. 275, 287, and *Alexander* v. *Worthington,* 5 Md. 471, 487.

much a part of the judgment of the court as is that on any other of the matters on which the case as a whole depends. The fact that the decision might have been placed upon a different ground existing in the case does not render a question expressly decided by the court a dictum."[14]

In support of this view are cited cases which ante-date the Dred Scott decision and others which, though, of later date, plainly purport to set forth long standing and established doctrine.[15] But logic too supports the same view of the matter. For the contrary view, by keeping open a choice by interested parties between the diverse grounds of decisions, would leave the law unsettled precisely in proportion as the courts had presumed to settle it.

Still it is urged that *constitutional* questions comprise a peculiar class of questions which should be left undecided if possible. To quote Justice Curtis's protest against the Chief Justice's opinion: "A great question of constitutional law, deeply affecting the peace and welfare of the country, is not . . . a fit subject to be thus reached"; such is the argument.[16] So far, however, is this alleged exception from being justified by the history of the matter, that it would be far nearer the truth to say that, if constitutional cases comprise a class by themselves in this reference, they warrant an exceptionally *broad* view of the legal value

[14] *Ib.*, 171. I am indebted for this reference to Albert W. R. Ewing's Legal and Historical Status of the Dred Scott Decision (Washington, 1909).

[15] See C. J. Waite in *R. R. Cos.* v. *Schutte*, 103 U. S. 118, cited with approval in *Union Pacific R. R. Co.* v. *Mason City, etc., R. R. Co.*, 199 U. S. 160.

[16] Rep. 590.

of judicial opinion. Let us consider as an example in this connection Chief Justice Marshall's decision in *Cohens* v. *Virginia.*[17]

In that case the plaintiff in error had been indicted and put to trial and penalty under a Virginia statute for selling tickets for a lottery which Congress had chartered for the District of Columbia. As in the Dred Scott case, the primary question before the court was one of jurisdiction, though in this case the Supreme Court's own jurisdiction, which counsel for Virginia denied upon the ground, among others, that a State was defendant contrary to the Eleventh Amendment. This objection Marshall met in the following terms: "It is, then, the opinion of the court, that the defendant who removes a judgment rendered against him by a State court into this court, for the purpose of examining the question whether that judgment be in violation of the Constitution or laws of the United States, does not commence or prosecute a suit against the State."[18] This utterance has from that day to the present been regarded as establishing the law on the point with which it deals,—and a vastly important point it plainly is.[19] Yet by the test set up by the critics of Chief Justice Taney's opinion in *Scott* v. *Sanford,* the utterance is not decisive; for its author continues thus: *"But should we in this be mistaken, the error does not affect the case now before the court,"* since plaintiff in error is not "a citizen of an-

[17] 6 Wheat. 264.

[18] *Ib.* 411-12.

[19] See, for example, *Holmes* v. *Jennison,* 14 Pet. 624 and *Prigg* v. *Pa.,* 16 Pet. 539; also, *Ableman* v. *Booth,* 21 How. 506.

other State" nor the "subject of any foreign State,"
but a citizen of Virginia herself.[20]

In short, the critics of Chief Justice Taney take
their view of the proper scope of judicial decisions
from a particular line of Common Law precedents
rather than from American Constitutional Law.
Altogether, the only feasible definition, historically,
of *obiter dictum* in the field of American Constitutional
Law would seem to be, a more or less casual utterance
by a court or members thereof upon some point not
deemed by the court itself to be strictly before it and
not necessary to decide, as preliminary to the determination of the controversy before it. Such an utterance, for example, is that of Chief Justice Marshall at
the close of his decision in *Brown* v. *Maryland,* where
he says that he "supposes" that the principles he has
just applied to a case arising in connection with foreign commerce would also apply in a case of commerce
among the States.[21] This pronouncement is obviously
an aside upon a point not argued before the Court and
it is quite justifiably ignored by Chief Justice Taney in
his opinion in the *License Cases,*[22] whereas the rest of
Marshall's opinion in *Brown* v. *Maryland* Taney treats
as law, though the entire second portion of it, dealing
with the "commerce" clause, was unnecessary, since
the immediate issue before the court had already been
disposed of under Article I, § 10, of the Constitution.

Chief Justice Taney had therefore, it appears, a
clear right to canvass the question of Dred's servitude

[20] See note 18.

[21] 12 Wheat, 419, 449.

[22] 5 How. 504, 574-578; see also J. McLean, *ib.* 594.

in support of his decision that Dred was not a citizen
of the United States, and he had the same right to
canvass the question of the constitutionality of the
Missouri Compromise in support of his decision that
Dred was a slave. To all these points his attention
was invited by arguments of counsel and to all of
them he might cast it with propriety by a well-estab-
lished view of the scope of judicial inquiry in such
matters. If then the decision rendered by six of the
nine judges on the bench, that the Missouri Compromise was unconstitutional, is to be stigmatized as un-
warrantable, which is all that the court of history can
do with it, it is not by pronouncing it to have been
obiter dictum but by discrediting, from the standpoint
of the history of Constitutional Law antedating the
decision, the principles upon which it was rested.

III

Turning then to consider the constitutional decision
directly, we find our task simplified to this extent:
that the entire court, majority and dissenting minority
alike, are in unanimous agreement upon the proposition that, whatever the source of its power, whether
Article IV, § 3 of the Constitution or the right to
acquire territory and therefore to govern it, Congress in governing territory is controlled by the Constitution—a proposition to which the court has always
adhered, though there has been latterly some alteration of opinion as to what provisions of the Constitution are applicable in this connection. And this was
the question that troubled the majority in the Dred
Scott case. The Missouri Compromise was unconsti-

tutional, that was certain; but just why—that was immensely uncertain.

The extremest position of all was taken by Justice Campbell, whose doctrine was that the only power Congress had in the territories, in addition to its powers as the legislature of the United States, was the power to make rules and regulations of a conservatory character "for the preservation of the public domain, and its preparation for sale or disposition." From this it was held to follow that whatever the Constitution and laws of the States "validly determine to be property, it is the duty of the Federal Government, through the domain of jurisdiction merely federal, to recognize to be property."[23] This of course was the extremest Calhounism, from which it came later to be deduced, with perfect logic, that it was the duty of the Federal Government, not only to admit slavery into the territory, but to protect it there. But, as Benton showed in his famous Examination of the Dred Scott Case, this particular phase of Calhounism was, at the date of the Dred Scott decision, less than ten years old.

But now it is a common view with historians, a view obviously traceable to Benton, that this decision rested *exclusively* upon Calhounist premises. Nothing could be farther from the fact. For though Justice Daniel of Virginia went almost as far as Justice Campbell in representing the power of Congress in governing the territories as a simple proprietary power of supervision, yet even he rejected Campbell's notion that Congress was the mere trustee of the States;

[23] Rep. 509-517; the quotations are from pp. 514 and 515.

while Justices Catron of Tennessee, an old Jacksonian Democrat, Grier of Pennsylvania and of similar traditions, Wayne, a Southern Whig, and the Chief Justice himself, could by no means consent thus to read the Constitution through the spectacles of the prophet of nullification. Upon what grounds then were these judges to rest their pronouncement of the unconstitutionality of the Compromise? Let us first take up the case of Catron and then turn to that of the Chief Justice, who spoke upon this point for himself, for Grier and Wayne, and to some extent for Daniel.

Catron paid his respects to the Calhounist point of view in the following words: "It is due to myself to say, that it is asking much of a judge, who has for nearly twenty years been exercising jurisdiction, from the western Missouri line to the Rocky Mountains, and, on this understanding of the Constitution," namely that Congress has power really to govern the territories, "inflicting the extreme penalty of death for crimes committed where the direct legislation of Congress was the only rule, to agree that he had been all the while acting in mistake, and as an usurper." Setting out from this extremely personal point of view, Catron found that Congress possessed *sovereignty* over its territory, limited however in this case by the treaty with France, with which the anti-slavery article of the Missouri Compromise was, he held, incompatible, and always by the "spirit" of the Constitution, which stipulates for the citizens of each State "the privileges and immunities of citizens in the several States."[24]

[24] Rep. 522-527.

A more extravagant line of reasoning it would be difficult to conceive. It is true that, at this date, the Supreme Court had not itself as yet had occasion to determine finally the legal effect of a congressional enactment in conflict with an earlier treaty, but the generally recognized doctrine was clearly that the treaty-making power could not prejudice Congress in the exercise of its granted powers; and this view had registered itself in reputable judicial decision only a few years before the Dred Scott decision, while to-day, of course, it is established law.[25]   But the appeal to Article IV, § 2, of the Constitution, significantly vague as it was, was even less warrantable.   All that this section of the Constitution was ever supposed to require was that no *State* should deny citizens of another State sojourning within its boundaries the *personal* rights of its own citizens,—*personal* rights, that is, as distinguished from *political* rights.[26]   Yet Catron seeks, not only to extend this provision to the powers of Congress, but also to make it guarantee citizens of States the rights enjoyed by them in their home States in every other State and territory of the Union!   One of Lincoln's criticisms of *Scott* v. *Sanford* was that logically it prohibited even the States from forbidding slavery within their respective limits. Restricted to Catron's opinion the criticism was valid.

But the most strongly nationalistic, or more precisely

[25] See the writer's National Supremacy (N. Y. 1913), 9-12 and references. The decision referred to was *Taylor* v. *Morton*, 2 Curt. 454 (1855). The law today is laid down in 112 U. S. 580 (1884), 122 *ib*. 116 (1887), 124 *ib*. 190 (1888), 130 *ib*. 581 (1889), 149 *ib*. 698 (1893).

[26] See Federalist No. 42, pp. 264-6 (Lodge's Ed.).

federalistic, of all the opinions upon the constitutional question was that of the Chief Justice, who, again following Marshall, traced the power of Congress to govern territories to its power to acquire them. Upon what ground then was he to rest his condemnation of the Missouri Compromise? In one or two passages Taney speaks of Congress as "trustee," but it is as trustee of the "whole *people* of the Union" and for *all* its powers. The limitations upon the power of Congress must therefore, in this case as in all cases, be sought in the Constitution, "from which it derives its own existence, and by virtue of which alone it continues to exist and act as a government and sovereignty." From this it follows that when Congress enters a territory of the United States it cannot "put off its character and assume discretionary or despotic powers which the Constitution has denied to it": it is still bound by the Constitution.[27] Therefore Congress can make no law for the territories with respect to establishing a religion, nor deny trial by jury therein, nor compel anyone to be a witness against himself in a criminal proceeding. "And," the Chief Justice continues,

"The rights of private property have been guarded with equal care." They "are united with the rights of persons

[27] Rep. 448-9. The italics are mine. Taney develops the doctrine that the U. S. can acquire territory *only* for the purpose of ultimately making States of it. This doctrine exactly reverses the argument, regarded sympathetically by Jefferson himself, against the validity of the La. Purchase: Henry Adams, History, II, chs. 4 and 5. Taney's opinion at this point was probably drawn in part from J. McKinley's opinion in *Pollard's Lessee* v. *Hagan,* 3 How. 212 (1845).

and placed on the same ground by the Fifth Amendment
to the Constitution, which provides that no person shall be
deprived of life, liberty and property without due process
of law. And an act of Congress which deprived a citizen
of the United States of his liberty or property merely
because he came himself or brought his property into a
particular territory of the United States, and who had
committed no offense against the laws, could hardly be
dignified with the name of due process of law. . . . The
powers over person and property of which we speak are
not only not granted to Congress, but are in express terms
denied. . . . And this prohibition is not confined to the
States, but the words are general and extend to the whole
territory over which the Constitution gives it power to
legislate. . . . It is a total absence of power everywhere
within the dominions of the United States, and places
the citizens of a territory, so far as these rights are
concerned, on the same footing with citizens of the
States. . . . And no word can be found in the Constitution which gives Congress a greater power over slave
property, or which entitles property of that kind to less
protection than property of any other description.   The
only power conferred is the power coupled with the duty
of guarding and protecting the owner in his rights."[28]

Undoubtedly it must be conceded at the outset that
in asserting for slave property a position within the
Constitution equal to that of any other kind of property, the Chief Justice was entirely in the right, his
Free Soil and Republican critics to the contrary notwithstanding. Their position, which was represented
for the nonce in Justice McLean's dissenting opinion,
was that there was a difference between slave property
and other kinds of property arising from the alleged
fact that slavery was contrary to natural law, and that
consequently, while the Constitution recognized prop-

[28] Rep. 450-1.

erty in slaves within the States where slavery was permitted, it did not recognize it within the territories. The argument was both erroneous and beside the point. Under our system of government title is acquired to property in nine cases out of ten under the jurisdiction of particular States and in accordance with the laws thereof, but once it has been so acquired, the subject-matter, whatever it be, is recognized by the Constitution as the property of its owner and his right to it as entitled to the protection of the Constitution.

But does this concession warrant the final sentence just quoted from the Chief Justice's opinion: "The only power conferred is the power coupled with the duty of guarding and protecting the owner in his rights"? Plainly not, unless, first, Congress must *always* assume a protective attitude toward *all* property in the exercise of *all* of its powers, or secondly, slave property occupied in 1857, not simply a position of *equality* with other property in the Constitution, but one of *superiority*. In behalf of the latter interpretation of his position, however, the Chief Justice offers not a word of proof. On the contrary, his whole argument is an implied disavowal of such an interpretation. Considering his repeated assertion that Congress is a sovereign legislature in the exercise of what powers belong to it, it seems clear that we can do his argument full justice only by treating it as tantamount to the proposition that Congress in the exercise of its powers has the same control of property, of whatever description, that any government would have in the exercise of the same powers, limited by the prohibitions of the Constitution in protection of property.

But what provision of the Constitution protective of the property right does the Chief Justice rely upon in this instance? As we have just seen, the "due process of law" clause of the Fifth Amendment. This, he recites, "provides that no person shall be deprived of life, liberty, and property, without due process of law. And," he comments, "an act of Congress which deprives a citizen of the United States of his liberty or property merely because he came himself or brought his property into a particular territory of the United States, and who had committed no offence against the laws could hardly be dignified with the name of due process of law."

At first approach there are two striking features to this argument, first, its apparent irrelevancy and secondly, its apparent begging of the question. It is admitted that property may be taken for "an offense against the laws," but it is implied that there has been no such offense. But this implication assumes the very point to be proved, namely, the unconstitutionality of the act of Congress under review. For if this was constitutional it was *law,* and an attempt to take slaves into a territory in contravention of it was "an offense against the *laws.*" And not less striking is the matter of irrelevancy. For to the lay mind the term "due process" suggests simply correct procedure, and in the Dred Scott case no question of procedure was involved, the antagonists of the Missouri Compromise being opposed, not to the method of its enforcement but to its enforcement at all, not to the *mode of its operation* but to its *substance*.

However, once we consult the Constitutional Law of the period, both these difficulties disappear and the question of the historical validity of Chief Justice Taney's argument stands before us on its merits.[29] Throughout the States in 1857, it was a generally acknowledged principle that there were certain limits beyond which legislative power was inherently incapable of proceeding in control of an owner's right to his property, that what the law once recognized to be property legislative power could not invade unduly. By the same date moreover, in some of the States, this principle had become established upon the "due process of law" and "law of the land" clauses of their respective constitutions.   And thus much for the supposed irrelevancy of the Chief Justice's argument. But by the same line of reasoning, the *petitio principii* pointed out therein also vanishes.   For if the due process clause prohibits legislation bearing with undue severity upon *existing* property rights, then all *new* legislation affecting such rights must be compared in this reference with the law which already defined those rights.   In other words, the term "laws" comes to mean the law as it stood *before* the new legislation was enacted; and "offenses against the laws" means offenses against *the law thus defined*.

What, then, in 1857, was that *undue severity* against

[29] For a fuller consideration of the subjects treated immediately below, see my articles in 24 Harv. Law Rev., 366 ffg., 460 ffg.

existing property rights which automatically con-
signed legislative acts to the wastebasket? To begin
with, every court in the country acknowledged that
private property could be taken by government for
only *public* uses, and further, that it could be so taken
only upon just compensation to the owner. But at
this point agreement ceased. In the years immediately
preceding the Dred Scott decision, many States passed
anti-liquor acts which, generally speaking, prohibited
not only the sale of intoxicating liquors save for medi-
cinal purposes and by licensed chemists, but also the
keeping of them, when not designed for this purpose,
elsewhere than in the dwelling of the owner; and such
acts applied equally to liquors *in existence at the moment of their going into effect* and to liquors to be
acquired in the future. In objection to them, accordingly, the argument soon began to be shaped, that
though they did not purpose to transfer to the State
outright the title to existing stocks of liquor, they
were in fact, in relation to these, *equivalent* to acts
of confiscation and void as such. Yet in twelve
States statutes of this description were upheld as
plainly within legislative power. Only in New York
in the case of *Wynehamer* v. *the People*,[30] was the act
of the legislature disallowed as contrary to the constitutional requirement of due process.

Now it is an interesting circumstance that the published briefs of counsel in *Scott* v. *Sanford* make no
reference to the Fifth Amendment.[31] And connected
with this circumstance is another not less interesting,

[30] 13 N. Y. 378 (1856).
[31] See Lawyer's Edition, Bk. XV, 691-8.

namely, that *Wynehamer* v. *the People* was decided
by the New York court of appeals at the very close of
the interval between the first and second argument of
Scott v. *Sanford*.   All things considered, there can be
little doubt that Chief Justice Taney took his doctrine
from the New York court of appeals.   Does then
Wynehamer v. *the People* furnish a precedent for
Scott v. *Sanford?*   Unquestionably it does, *if we assume that there was already slave property in the*
*territory governed by the eighth section of the Mis-
souri Compromise at the date of its enactment.*   But
this, the Chief Justice does not attempt to show, nor
indeed, does he mention the point.   Also this consideration would not, *necessarily* certainly, have affected
the validity of the Compromise as to slave property
brought into the territory at a later date.   But finally,
even if we give this precedent its widest possible operation, *yet it represented the doctrine of a single State
and was in flat conflict with the doctrine of a full
dozen other States.*

But now let us recall once more the acknowledged
purpose of the court in entering upon the constitutional question in *Scott* v. *Sanford*.   It was to settle
the question of Congress' power over slavery in the
territories,—which meant, however, not Congress'
power over slavery actually existing in the territories,
but its power to prevent slaves from being brought
into the territories *henceforth*.   And on this question
the New York precedent throws not the least light.
Two of the judges in the Wynehamer case expressed
the opinion that the withdrawal of the right of sale

from subsisting owners would alone suffice to invalidate a legislative act, but the other judges gave no countenance to this doctrine, and the court itself later formally disavowed it. The decision in the case is based solely on the proposition that the total effect of the act before the court was the *destruction* of certain existing property. But for the Chief Justice to have contended that the prohibition by Congress of slavery in the territories effected anything like a destruction of existing slave property outside the territories would have been absurd in the extreme, nor in fact does he venture to hint such a notion.

The only purpose of the Missouri Compromise and of later acts of Congress of the same character, *and their only effect,* was to withdraw from owners outside the territories governed by them the right to enter there with their slaves. Viewed in this light there can be no doubt that so far as available Constitutional Law stood in 1857, these acts were entirely valid under the Fifth Amendment. Otherwise, as Justice Curtis inquired in his dissenting opinion, what was to be said of the Ordinance of 1787, which Virginia and other States had ratified notwithstanding the presence of similar clauses in their constitutions? What again was to be said, upon that hypothesis, of the act of Virginia herself, passed in 1778, which prohibited the further importation of slaves? What was to be said of numerous decisions in which this and analogous laws had been upheld and enforced by the courts of Maryland and Virginia, against their own citizens who had purchased slaves abroad, and that without anyone's thinking to question the validity of such laws on the ground that they were not law of the land or due process of law? What was to be said of the act of Congress of 1808 prohibiting the slave trade and the assumption of the Constitution that Congress would have that power without its being specifically bestowed, but simply as an item of its power to regulate commerce? What finally, if the scope of congressional authority to legislate was thus limited by the Fifth Amendment, was to be said of the Embargo Act, which had borne with peculiar severity upon the people of the New England States, but the constitutionality of which had been recently asserted by the court in argument in the roundest terms.[32]

Nonetheless, subsequent developments in our constitutional jurisprudence prove that Taney chose his ground in *Scott* v. *Sanford* with some prescience. Indeed, even before the War, the Republican critics of the decision, instead of utilizing Curtis's very effective

[32] Rep. 626-627; the Virginia cases cited are 5 Call 425 and 1 Leigh 172, and the Maryland case is 5 Harr. and J. 107. The learned justice might have added 2 Munf. (Va.) 393. The case in which the Embargo Act was adverted to was *U. S.* v. *Marigold,* 9 How. 560, in which the court upheld an act of Congress prohibiting the importation of fraudulent coins. Justice Curtis should also have inquired how, upon the Chief Justice's argument, Congress had power to exclude goods purchased by American citizens abroad "merely because" the duty had not been paid on them. See also C. J. Marshall in *Gibbons* v. *Ogden,* 9 Wheat. 1, 196-7 (1821), where the doctrine is stated that the only limitations to the power of Congress is regulating foreign and interstate commerce are the purely political limitations which arise from the responsibility of Congress to its constituents. See also Fed. Nos. 23 and 33, for similar doctrine as to some other powers of Congress.

dissent at this point, themselves pounced upon the Fifth Amendment and by emphasizing the word "liberty" in it, instead of the word "property," based upon it the dogma that Congress could not *allow* slavery in the territories.[33] After the Civil War Taney's Republican successor, Chase, invoked the Amendment in his opinion in *Hepburn* v. *Griswold* in the same sense in which Taney had invoked it, but only as a limitation upon the *implied* powers of Congress.[34] This doctrine was flatly rejected by the court itself, speaking through Justice Strong, in *Knox* v. *Lee.*[35] Yet a few years later, Strong too was elaborating the Taney-Chase point of view in his dissenting opinion in the Sinking Fund cases,[36] and connecting it with the early New York and North Carolina precedents.

But of course, the most noteworthy applications of the *doctrine* of Due Process of Law have been made by the courts in their interpretation of the Fourteenth Amendment, the terms "liberty" and "property" in

[33] See the Republican Platform of 1860, par. 8. At this point the Republicans followed McLean's opinion rather than Curtis's. Note the significance in this connection of the discussion as to whether slavery was recognized by the Constitution; and also of the discussion as to whether it was recognized by natural law.

[34] 8 Wall. 603, 624; see J. Miller's cogent answer, ib. 637-638. Also, see the Chief Justice's own decision in *Veazie Bank* v. *Fenno* in the same volume of reports, 533 ffg.

[35] 12 Wall. 457, 551. C. J. Chase elaborates upon his earlier argument under the Fifth Amendment at 580-582.

[36] 99 U. S. 700, 737-739. See also the various justices in the Northern Securities Company case, 193 U. S. 197, 332, 362, 397-400. See also J. Harlan in *Adair* v. *United States,* 208 U. S. 161, 172-174; *cf.* J. McKenna, ib. 180-190, and J. Holmes, 191.

which are to-day given a very extended significance. This development, however, has been matched by the *pari passu* development of the doctrine that legislative power extends, generally speaking, to the enactment of all *reasonable* laws and that such laws *are* "due process." The legislative stagnation that the earlier doctrine logically imported has thus been obviated. But at the same time, we have to give the Dred Scott case a place in the line of precedents from which has finally emerged one of the most fruitful doctrines of modern Constitutional Law.[37]

IV

But there is one other topic worth our brief consideration before closing this paper, namely, the character of the issue between Chief Justice Taney and Justice Curtis upon the question of citizenship raised by Dred's attempt to sue in the federal courts. The usual view of the issue referred to is that it resolved itself into a dispute as to whether negroes were *in any case* capable of citizenship at the time of the adoption of the Constitution. This account of the matter is inaccurate. A careful comparison of Chief Justice Taney's opinion with that of Justice Curtis reveals the fact that the fundamental issue between the two, though it is not very specifically joined, is not whether there may not have been negro citizens of States in 1787 who upon the adoption of the Constitution became citizens of the United States, but from what source citizenship within the recognition of the Consti-

[37] See the present writer in 7 Mich. Law Rev. 642 ffg.

tution was supposed to flow *thenceforth*. Upon this point, Curtis's view was that citizenship within the recognition of the Constitution in the case of persons born within the United States was through the States, while Taney's view was that a "citizen of the United States," to use his frequent phrase, always, unless descended from those who became citizens at the time of the adoption of the Constitution, owed his character as such to some intervention of national authority—was, in short, a product of the National Government.[38] Curtis's theory, it can hardly be doubted, was that of the framers of the Constitution, wherefore Taney's pretense of carrying out not only the spirit but the very letter of the Constitution as it came from the framers, becomes at this point particularly hollow.[39] On the other hand, Taney's view is a very logical, and indeed inevitable, deduction from his whole body of doctrine with reference to the dual nature of the federal system: the States independent and sovereign within their sphere and the National Government within its. This theory Taney had voiced from the beginning of his judicial career, so that, at this point he was at least acting consistently with his past. Also, without doubt, the doctrine in question was pretty well

[38] Taney states his position on this point at pp. 404-406 and 417-422 of the Report, and Curtis states his at p. 581.

[39] Taney translates the "citizens of each State" clause of the Constitution as "citizens of the United States," but the derivation of this clause from the Articles of Confederation forbids any such notion. The original source of the Chief Justice's argument on the citizenship question is to be found in Reports of Committees, No. 80, 27th Congress, 3rd session, a very instructive document.

established by 1857, both in judicial decision and in political thinking.[40]

.   .   .   .

To summarize: I conclude, first, that the Dred Scott decision was not *obiter dictum* within any definition of *obiter dictum* obtainable from a fair review of the practice of the Supreme Court, particularly under Marshall, in constitutional cases; secondly, that it was not based by the majority of those entering into it upon Calhounist premises; and thirdly, that Justice Curtis's supposed refutation of Taney's argument upon the question of Dred's title to a *prima facie* citizenship within the recognition of the Constitution is a fiction. None of these results, however, goes far to relieve that decision of its discreditable character as a judicial utterance. When, as in this case, the student finds six judges arriving at precisely the same result by three distinct processes of reasoning, he is naturally disposed to surmise that the result may possibly have induced the processes rather than that the processes compelled the result, though of course such surmise is not necessarily sound; but when he discovers further that the processes themselves were most deficient in that regard for history and precedent in which judicial reasoning is supposed to abound, his surmise becomes suspicion; and finally when he finds that beyond reasoning defectively upon the matter before

[40] For a good statement of this doctrine, see Taney's opinion in *Ableman* v. *Booth*, cited *supra* in note 19. *It should be noted in passing that this elucidation of the real issue between Taney and Curtis on the citizenship question throws additional light on the close relation existing in Taney's mind between the question of Dred's servitude and that of his citizenship.*

them, the same judges deliberately gloss over material distinctions (as for example, in this case, the distinction between sojourn and domicile) and ignore precedents that they have themselves created (as for example, in this case, the decisions regarding the operation of State decisions upon questions of comity) his suspicion becomes conviction. The Dred Scott decision cannot be, with accuracy, written down as usurpation, but it can and must be written down as a gross abuse of trust by the body which rendered it. The results from that abuse of trust were moreover momentous. During neither the Civil War nor the period of Reconstruction did the Supreme Court play anything like its due rôle of supervision, with the result that during the one period the military powers of the President underwent undue expansion, and during the other the legislative powers of Congress. The court itself was conscious of its weakness, yet notwithstanding its prudent disposition to remain in the background, at no time since Jefferson's first administration has its independence been in greater jeopardy than in the decade between 1860 and 1870; so slow and laborious was its task of recuperating its shattered reputation.

SOME POSSIBILITIES IN THE WAY
OF TREATY-MAKING

SOME POSSIBILITIES IN THE WAY OF TREATY-MAKING [1]

Under date of September 26, 1906, seven European nations entered into a treaty by which they agreed to prohibit within their respective dominions night work for women, and into another treaty by which they similarly agreed to prohibit the use of white phosphorus in the manufacture of matches. These same countries have also entered into treaties with regard to the insurance of workmen against industrial accidents. Lastly, proposals which have already been formulated are to be submitted in September of the present year for an international agreement prohibiting the night work of young persons and fixing the maximum working day for women and young persons. The question arises, why, if other countries may enter into and carry into effect such engagements, may not the United States?

The powers of the National Government, though enumerated, are each of them sovereign powers and keep pace in their development with the enlargement of the subject-matter amenable to them. Said the court in *South Carolina* v. *the United States:*

"The Constitution is a written instrument. As such its meaning does not alter, and what it meant when adopted it means now. Being a grant of powers to a government,

[1] The following paper was read at the 20th annual meeting of the Lake Mohawk Conference on International Arbitration, May 28, 1914.

its language is general, and as changes come in social and political life, it embraces in its grasp all new conditions which are within the scope of the powers in terms conferred. In other words, while the powers granted do not change, they apply from generation to generation to all things to which they are in their nature applicable."[2]

With the growth of international trade relations, immigration, and other forms of international intercourse, the conditions of life within particular nations become of ever increasing concern to their neighbors, with the result that treaty-making among the independent states of the world tends to extend to matters earlier deemed to lie quite without its sphere. In this general development the United States must and does participate and for the resultant legal responsibilities the powers of the National Government are, if we adhere to the historically settled canons of Constitutional Law bearing on the subject, entirely adequate. In the words of Chief Justice Marshall: "The Constitution [was] intended to endure for ages and consequently to be adapted to the various crises of human affairs."[3]

[2] 199 U. S. 437, 448-9. See also J. Moody in *Ill. Cent. R. R. Co.* v. *Howard*, 207 U. S. 463, 520: "It is said that Congress has never before enacted legislation of this nature for the government of interstate commerce by land . . . The fundamental fallacy of this argument is that it misunderstands the nature of the Constitution . . . and forgets that its unchanging provisions are adaptable to the infinite variety of the changing conditions of our national life." C. J. Waite's well-known utterance in the *Pensacola Tel. Co.* v. *the Western Un. Tel. Co.* 96 U. S. 1, should also be recalled in this connection.

[3] 4 Wheat. 316, 415. Note also his words in the same place, p. 407: "We cannot comprehend the train of reasoning which would maintain that the extent of power granted by the people

But it will be objected that the regulation of the hours and conditions of labor falls in the United States to what is called the "police powers" of the States. This is true, but that fact does not withdraw the same subject from regulation by the National Government in the *bona fide* exercise of *its* powers. The National Government has only certain enumerated powers, but it may exercise these powers for all the legitimate purposes of government that events may bring within their reach. A like objection to the one just recited was made to the recent Mann Act forbidding the transportation of women from one State to another for immoral purposes. This, said the objectors, did not regulate commerce among the States for *commercial* purposes, but for *moral* purposes, and so invaded the power of the States to regulate the public morals. But Justice McKenna, speaking for the unanimous Court, replied:

"Our dual form of government has its perplexities, State and Nation having different spheres of jurisdiction, but it must be kept in mind that we are one people; and the powers reserved to the States and those conferred on the Nation are adapted to be exercised, whether independently or concurrently, to promote the general welfare, material and moral."[4]

is to be ascertained, not by the nature and terms of the grant, but by its date." Note also the words of J. Story in *Martin* v. *Hunter's Lessee,* 1 Wheat. 304, 326: "The Constitution unavoidably deals in general language. . . . The instrument was not intended to provide merely for the exigencies of a few years, but was to endure through a long lapse of ages, the events of which were locked up in the inscrutable purposes of Providence." These words are quoted less as stating a rule of law, however, than as indicating the point of view from which the Constitution *must* be construed if it is to last.

[4] 227 U. S. 308, 322.

The utterance is in the very spirit of the words of the Preamble of the Constitution.

Suppose, however, that the action taken by the National Government *conflicts* with that taken by the State with reference to the same subject-matter? The pertinent provision of the Constitution is undoubtedly Art. VI, par. 2:

"This Constitution, the acts of Congress in pursuance thereof, and the treaties made or which shall be made under the authority of the United States, are the supreme law of the land; and the judges of each State shall be bound thereby, anything in the constitution or laws of any State to the contrary notwithstanding."

Words could not be plainer than these, especially when they are given their historical setting.

The Convention of 1787 desired nothing so much as to get rid of that State intervention which had wrecked the Articles of Confederation. This it accomplished in four ways: 1—By referring the Constitution to the People; 2—By providing the National Government with executive machinery of its own; 3—By making the national Supreme Court the final interpreter of the Constitution; 4—By providing for the supremacy in *all* cases of national authority as defined by the Constitution over conflicting State authority. The point of view of the Convention was voiced by Wilson thus: "With respect to the province and object of the General Government they [the States] should be considered as having no existence."[5]

[5] See Madison's Notes, under date of June 25. Equally to the point was Read of Delaware's earlier objection to a proposition that the U. S. should guarantee the several States in their territory: "It abetted the idea of distinct States, which would

Later a motion was offered in the Convention prohibiting the National Government "to interfere with the government of the individual States in any matter of internal police which respects the government of such State only and wherein the general welfare of the United States is not concerned." Despite the careful language in which it was couched the motion was voted down by eight States to two.[6]

The view that the reserved powers of the States comprise an independent limitation on national power probably found expression for the first time in the debate on Hamilton's Bank Project of 1791. Opposed as he was to the Bank, Madison pronounced the argument fallacious: *"Interference with the powers of the States,"* said he, *"was no constitutional criterion of the power of Congress.* If the power was not given, Congress could not exercise it; if given, they might exercise it, although it should interfere with the laws or even the constitution of the States."[7]

Nevertheless, a generation later the same notion was again afoot. "It has been contended," recites Chief Justice Marshall in his opinion in *Gibbons* v. *Ogden,* "that if a law passed by a State in the exercise of its acknowledged sovereignty comes into conflict with a law passed by Congress in pursuance of the Constitu-

be a perpetual source of discord." The proposition was then altered to the present guaranty of "a republican form of government" and was agreed to, *nem. con.: ib.* under date of June 11. Considering the fact that territorial cessions so often furnish the purpose of treaties, the refusal of the Convention to make the guarantee in question is particularly significant.

    Loc. cit. under date of July 17.

[7] Annals of Cong. II, col. 1891. The emphasis is mine.

tion, they affect the subject and each other like equal and opposing powers." "But," the Chief-Justice answered,

"The framers of our Constitution foresaw this state of things and provided for it, by declaring the supremacy not only of itself but of the laws made in pursuance of it. The nullity of any act inconsistent with the Constitution is produced by the declaration that the Constitution is the supreme law. The appropriate application of that part of the clause which confers the same supremacy on laws and treaties is to such acts of State legislatures as do not transcend their powers, but, though enacted in the execution of acknowledged State powers, interfere with, or are contrary to the laws of Congress made in pursuance of the Constitution, or some treaty made under the authority of the United States. In every such case, the act of Congress or the treaty is supreme; and the law of the State, though enacted in the exercise of powers not controverted, must yield to it."[8]

I admit that with the advance of the dissolving theories of the Great Nullifier, in the period between the death of Marshall and the Civil War, the doctrine of *Gibbons* v. *Ogden* was temporarily abandoned for the view that State power comprised of itself a limitation upon national power. Indeed, this view is, after all, but a particular form of Calhoun's doctrine. For while the actual business of nullifying national authority is farmed out, so to say, with the Supreme Court, the pretended basis of the power, namely, the vast, undefined powers of the States, remains the same.

But the crucial fact is that the Supreme Court has to-day returned to first principles. Of this such decisions as those in *Henderson* v. *New York*,[9] *in re*

[8] 9 Wheat. 1, 210-11 (1824). The emphasis is mine.
[9] 92 U. S. 279 (1875).

Rahrer,[10] the recent *Employers' Liability Cases*,[11] and *Minnesota Rate Cases*,[12] furnish proof positive, to say nothing of a host of dicta.

Thus in the Employers' Liability Cases, the court was confronted with the now notorious decision of Chief Justice Baldwin of the Connecticut supreme court in the Hoxie case, in which enforcement had been refused the act of Congress on the ground of its disharmony with "the policy of the State." Strangely unaware as the Connecticut court showed itself to be of the established canons of Constitutional Law, its view must after all be admitted to have been the inevitable one if the reserved powers of the States limit national power. But, as I say, the Supreme Court of the United States no longer subscribes to this doctrine. The theory of the Connecticut court was accordingly swept aside, in the following words taken from the court's earlier opinion in *Smith* v. *Alabama*:

"The grant of power to Congress to regulate commerce . . . is paramount over all legislative powers which, in consequence of not having been granted to Congress, are reserved to the States. It follows that any legislation of a State, although in pursuance of an acknowledged power reserved to it, which conflicts with the actual exercise of the power of Congress over the subject of commerce, must give way before the supremacy of the national authority."[13]

In the *Minnesota Rate Cases* the Court invited Con-

---

[10] 142 U. S. 545 (1891).

[11] *Mondou* v. *N. Y., N. H., and H. R. R. Co* v. *U. S.* 223 U. S.

[12] *Simpson* v. *Shephard* 230 U. S. 352.

[13] 124 U. S. 465, 473 (1888).

gress to take over the business of regulating infra-
State rates so far as might be necessary and proper
to make effective its regulation of inter-State rates.[14]

And, as Marshall's words just quoted, indicate,
the principles that determine the relation of Congress'
power to State power also determine the relation of
the national treaty-making power to State power.
Certainly, no power falls more distinctly within the
reserved powers of the States than the power to regulate the tenure of real property. In this connection,
note the language of Justice Field in *United States*
v. *Fox*:

"The power of the State to regulate the tenure of real
property within her limits, and the modes of its acqui-
sition and transfer, and the rules of its descent, and the
extent to which testamentary disposition of it may be
exercised by its owner, is undoubted."[15]

And again the language of Justice Washington in
McCormick v. *Sullivant*:

"The title and modes of disposition of real property
within the States, whether *inter vivos* or testamentary,
are not matters placed under the control of federal
authority."[16]

Yet the same judges, with one exception, who
decided the McCormick case also decided *Chirac* v.
Chirac[17]; the same judges, with one exception, who
decided *United States* v. *Fox* also decided *Hauenstein*
v. *Lynham*[18]; and the judge who wrote the opinion in

[14] See especially J. Hughes' language at p. 399 of the Report.
[15] 94 U. S. 315, 320.
[16] 10 Wheat. 192, 202.
[17] 2 Wheat. 259 (1817).
[18] 100 U. S. 483 (1879).

the *United States* v. *Fox* again spoke for the court in *Geofroy* v. *Riggs*.[19]   In each of these three cases the issue was the same; it lay between claimants to real estate whose right to the property involved was admitted to be perfect under the local law and other claimants who asserted the right to claim the same property *as heirs* to it upon the basis of certain treaty provisions.   In each case the decision of the United States Supreme Court, given unanimously, was in favor of the latter claimants; and the basis of the decision was in each case announced to be Article VI, par. 2.   Later, reviewing these and similar decisions, Attorney-General Griggs stated the rule that they unmistakably establish: *"The fact that a treaty provision annuls and supersedes the law of a particular State upon the same subject is no objection to the validity of the treaty."*[20]

In a word, what powers the States possess is a matter of the utmost indifference in determining the scope of the treaty-making power of the United States.   Or to put it otherwise, the United States has exactly the same range of power in making treaties that it would have if the States did not exist.[21] *Let a matter arise that is of genuine international concern and the na-*

[19] 133 U. S. 258 (1890).

[20] 22 Opins. Atty. Gen'l 214.

[21] Of course the U. S. cannot, in view of its obligation to guarantee the States "a republican form of government" assume to control and direct the actual machinery of government within the States indefinitely.   But that fact does not detract from the force of the statement in the text.   For if there were no States, there would be no such machinery of government to control and direct to any extent.

*tional power to negotiate treaties with reference to it
and to give those treaties the force and effect of law
of the land becomes perfected.*

At the present moment, I am informed from re-
liable sources, an agreement is in process of negotiation
with the Dominion of Canada which will have for its
purpose the extension of the provisions of the recent
Weeks-McLean Migratory Bird Law to the case of
birds passing from Canada. It would be difficult to
distinguish such a treaty in principle from one of the
sort mentioned at the opening of this paper, for the
State's police power with reference to its wild game is
well settled.[22]   The precedent will be the more precious
from its origin with a State-rights Administration.

---

[22] See *e.g., Geer* v. *Conn.* 161 U. S. 519. Mr. Henry Chase in his
recent volume on Game Protection seems to think that while the
Weeks-McLean Act is possibly unconstitutional as invading the
police powers of the States, a treaty covering the same matter
would not be open to this objection.   That is a great
mistake. If the reserved powers of the States restrict Congress
in the exercise of its powers, then also do they restrict the
national treaty-making power in its capacity to make "law of
the land".   My own belief is that the Weeks-McLean
Act is perfectly constitutional as an act "necessary and
proper" to protect the federal timber reserves.   The act is
analogous to congressional legislation intended to repress
crime within districts subject to Congress' exclusive power of
legislation.   The authors of crimes committed within such districts, forts, arsenals, etc., are often tried outside them, within
State territory.   But if a resident of a State should attempt to
rescue the culprit in such a case he would be subject to federal
law.   Likewise, if a resident of a State should withhold information with reference to a crime committed within a district subject
to Congress' exclusive power, he would be guilty, under the
act of Congress, of misprision of felony, and punishable there-
for.   And examples might be multiplied: *Cohens* v. *Va.* 6

The whole question, then, is wrapped up in the phrase "genuine international concern," and this, as I have indicated, is a thing ever advancing and developing. What with cable, steamship, wireless telegraphy, and inter-oceanic canals, the world to-day is astonishingly small and the consequence is that the nations can no longer live unto themselves in the way that was earlier possible. The rise of an international police power and of an international power of eminent domain, exercisable by the fitter members in the Family of Nations, is a development clear and palpable before our eyes. The development of uniform national legislation of social character, in pursuance of international agreement, is but another phase of the broader development of international solidarity.

And it is the fundamental contention of this paper that the United States is competent to march abreast of this development.[23]

Wheat. 264, 424-30. Congress, whatever of its powers it happens to be exercising at any particular moment, is always the national legislature, and capable as such of giving its acts nation-wide operation,—so that they be passed in exercise of its constitutional powers. The only question with reference to the Migratory Bird Act is, then, whether its nation-wide operation is a necessary and proper measure for the protection of national property of great value. Certainly, there can be no dispute about that. The efforts of the advocates of the law, however, to bring it within the "commerce" clause seem to me rather far-fetched.

[23] For further discussion of the questions above considered, see the writer's National Supremacy (Holt and Co., N. Y., 1913); also, his article on the Treaty-Making Power in the North Am. Rev. for June, 1914.

INDEX

(The list of cases indexed is incomplete.)

173